THE ANIMAL ADVENTURER'S GUIDE

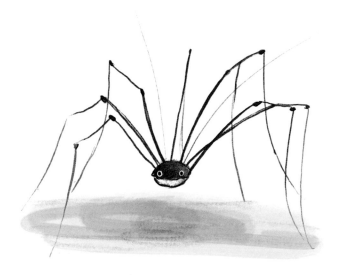

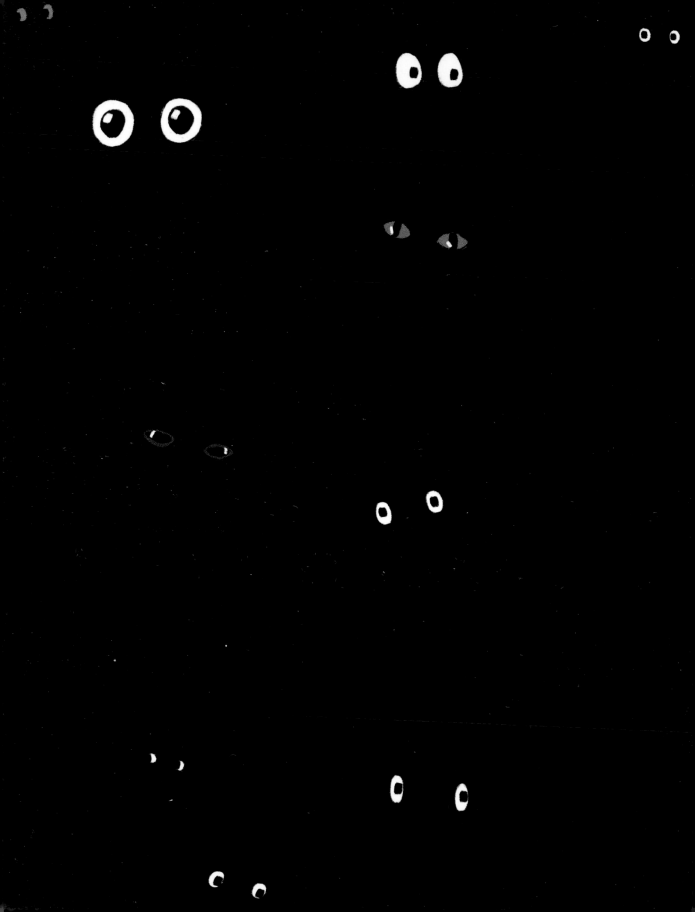

THE ANIMAL ADVENTURER'S GUIDE

HOW TO PROWL FOR AN OWL, MAKE SNAIL SLIME, AND CATCH A FROG BARE-HANDED

50 ACTIVITIES TO GET WILD WITH ANIMALS

SUSIE SPIKOL   ILLUSTRATED BY BECCA HALL

ROOST BOOKS

RIBBIT!

To my mother and father, who always
encouraged me to find the tracks and
follow my heart and to the Harris Center for
Conservation Education where the tracks
have led me and my heart has mattered

Contents

WILD IS RIGHT HERE

One warm summer night, not too long ago, I went up to the garden. Something small was eating the carrot greens just as they were pressing their way out of the soft ground. A glistening track of silver, sparkling in my flashlight, caught my eye. It shimmered, leading me through a tangle of eaten vegetables. And then it happened: I fell in love with a snail.

A small brown snail was bending my garden greens and engulfing my seedlings. I picked up the penny-sized creature. Cradling it in my palm, I held my breath, waiting for it to feel brave enough to peek out from its spiraled shell. Slowly, so slowly, I felt the snail's cool foot slide out against my skin. I watched as it lifted its long, antennae-like tentacles. At the tip of each tentacle sat an eye, taking me in. On that warm June night, I sat in the garden holding that tiny snail and—I did—I fell in love with it.

It isn't so unusual for some small, unsuspecting creature to capture my heart—toads, bumblebees, salamanders, red velvet mites, star-nosed moles, woolly bear caterpillars have done it before.

This is why I get along so well with the children I teach. We stop and notice. We lean into the things we find. Our eyes are open, our hands outstretched. Once, I watched a young boy encounter a milkweed tussock moth caterpillar. He was holding it up to his nose and sniffing it. He said, "It smells just like me when I've been outside all day." Of course, I had to sniff it too. He was right.

The small things in nature—the things we can hold, touch, or lie down next to and watch closely—these are the things that open our hearts as children. These are what remind us of our connection to one another. When we stretch out a gentle finger in invitation to the snail, the worm, the caterpillar, the dragonfly, we know—even from, and perhaps especially from, a young age—that we are both alive in this one moment together.

Stop and open your eyes, shift your perception. There are wild animals all around us almost every moment of every day. Whether it's hearing the blue jays' call or catching little brown toads, everyday creatures are waiting to wake up your and your child's curiosity and sense of wonder. Start small and think local when it comes to offering and exposing your children to opportunities to wildlife. We have everything we need in our own neighborhoods to get started falling in love with this world and what it has to offer.

SNAIL

LET'S GET WILD

Are you an animal person? Do you find bears, butterflies, or turtles more interesting than people? If holding a frog, humming to a snail, following a fox track, or hooting to an owl are things you'd like to do, you've come to right place. Read on and discover secret tried-and-true steps to uncovering the world of the everyday wild creatures in your own neighborhood. No matter where you live, animals live there too, and you only need to know a few simple things to start exploring.

TIPS

* **Pay attention!** Wild animals are all around us. Slowing down, tuning in, and being quiet will help you notice them. Don't forget the tiny things, like the red velvet mite, who is even smaller than the head of a pin, or the jewellike hummingbirds of your world. Every animal is someone to meet.

* **Practice kindness.** Animals are living, breathing creatures, just like you. When you have the chance to be up close and connect with them, be just as kind and friendly as you would if you were meeting a person.

* **Safety first.** Your animal adventures will have you exploring at dawn, dusk, and night. No matter where or when you are going, always let a grown-up know. If you go on a night adventure, bring along a grown-up. Also, practice personal safety by paying attention to your surroundings and making sure the animals you are searching for aren't a danger to you.

* **Leave it better than you found it.** Keep the natural world full of nature, not your trash or food. If an animal visited your house, you wouldn't want them to trash it, right? So, treat wherever you go with the same respect.

* **Gear up.** This won't require fancy equipment, but it helps to have a few essentials things in a backpack, ready to go when you hear that a snake has been spotted in your neighborhood or an owl is hooting out your door.

TOP 10 THINGS TO HAVE IN YOUR PACK

(1) BINOCULARS (PURCHASED OR DIY; SEE ACROSS)

(2) *YOUR FIELD JOURNAL

(3) 1–2 PENCILS

(4) RULER

(5) MAGNIFYING LENS

(6) PLASTIC BAGS FOR COLLECTING THINGS LIKE FUR, BONES, AND POOP

(7) RUBBER, LATEX, OR PLASTIC GLOVES

(8) FLASHLIGHT

(9) FIELD GUIDES FOR YOUR AREA ON TOPICS LIKE BIRDS, ANIMAL TRACKS, AND AMPHIBIANS AND REPTILES

(10) CAMERA (OPTIONAL)

*Note: Your field journal doesn't need to be fancy—just a notebook where you can write down your observations, record your finds, and map and sketch what you see.

You will also notice that there are specific lists of materials you will need, for each of the activities in this book.

DIY TUBE BINOCULARS

Binoculars are a great tool for watching animals, from birds and butterflies to chipmunks and whales, because they let you see what is far away and help your eyes focus on the animal. If you have a pair, that's great! If you don't, you can make your own. Even though they won't make the faraway creatures look closer, these simple tube binoculars will really help your eyes focus on the animals you see.

THINGS YOU'LL NEED

2 cardboard tubes
or toilet paper rolls

Duct tape, any color

Stickers (optional)

Hole punch

Ribbon, string, or yarn

1   Line up the tubes next to each other lengthwise and wrap the duct tape around the tubes to form a binocular shape.

2   Decorate them with stickers to give them your own style, if you want.

3   Punch a hole on the outside edge of each tube.

4   Tie a strand of ribbon, string, or yarn through the punched holes to make a loop big enough to fit over your head. The binoculars should hang down to the middle of your chest.

5   Try them out!

BLUE JAY

CARDINAL

BIRDS

FEATHERS, BEAKS, TALONS, AND SONGS

ACTIVITIES

Birds have captured our imaginations since ancient times. Covered in brilliant feathers and powered by wings, they can do astounding things—from singing sweet melodies and building nests to migrating thousands of miles and soaring to great heights. No matter where you live, there are always birds to be seen and heard.

Find out how to get up close to these dinosaur descendants and even have them eating out of your hands. Discover how to be a bird spy, build a camouflage shelter, talk to chickadees, call in owls, and even dissect a pellet of bird barf. Stretch your mind and wings and take off with the birds!

PIGEON

OWL

SPY ON A BIRD

A.K.A. BIRD WATCHING

Have you ever wanted to be a spy? Well, learning how to watch birds is like becoming a spy. You have to be sneaky, quiet, and clever, and stay hidden. Birds are smarter than you think: if they spy you before you spy them, your cover will be blown and they will fly away. Your mission, if you choose to accept it, is to see how many birds you can spy in your neighborhood.

THINGS YOU'LL NEED

Natural-colored and quiet-sounding clothes

Binoculars (optional)

Field guide to birds in your area

Field journal

Pencil

SKILLS YOU'LL LEARN

Observing

Comparing

Describing

Drawing

Identifying

1   Dress for success! To be a bird spy, you will want to wear clothes that give you good camouflage outside—think browns, grays, dark greens, and black. Also, you want your outfit to be as quiet as possible. When you move, does your clothing make any noise? Birds are always paying attention. If they see or hear you, they will fly away before you get to see them.

2   The early bird spy catches the . . . bird! Birds are most active in early morning, so if you want to see a lot of birds, head out right after sunrise. But that doesn't mean this is the only time to see birds. If you are super observant, you can find birds any time of the day.

3   Get your bird eyes and ears on! You will need to be extra sharp-eyed and sharp-eared. Look for movement in trees, shrubs, power lines, and grasses, and listen for their chirps, trills, and songs.

4   Mission accomplished! When you see a bird, quiet your body and get as still as possible. You don't need binoculars, but if you have them or you've made a pair of homemade binoculars (see "DIY Tube Binoculars" on page 3), use them

to focus on a bird. Be observant and see what details you can notice about it, such as:

* HOW BIG IS IT?

* WHAT COLORS STAND OUT?

* WHAT SHAPE IS ITS BEAK?

* WHAT IS IT DOING?

* BASED ON WHAT YOU NOTICE ABOUT HOW THE BIRD LOOKS AND WHAT IT IS DOING, WHAT WOULD YOU NAME IT?

* USING A FIELD GUIDE, CAN YOU IDENTIFY IT?

5 Use your field journal to answer these questions and draw sketches.

BIRD SPIES!

Did you know that birds have actually been trained to be real spies? During World Wars I and II, some birds were masters of espionage. Homing pigeons were trained to deliver messages to troops close to enemy lines. They were also outfitted with tiny cameras strapped to their bodies so they could collect important information about rival troops. During the Cold War, ravens and crows, known for their high intelligence, were taught to deposit listening devices on window ledges. These birds even snapped a few photographs with specially designed cameras that were held inside their beaks. So next time you are spying on birds, remember: maybe, just maybe, they are also spying on you!

BUILD A BIRD BLIND

Imagine if you could see birds but they couldn't see you! Then you'd really be able to watch their behavior. Maybe you'd see a robin eat a worm like a piece of spaghetti or a blue jay tuck away a seed for the winter or a phoebe build its nest. You may also see other animals, like chipmunks and squirrels.

You can go invisible like a real professional wildlife watcher by building a simple blind, also known as a bird hide. A *blind* is a shelter that camouflages you so you are hidden from view. Wildlife biologists and photographers often use blinds to get their best work done. Get ready to slip on your invisibility cloak and see into the secret lives of birds and other animals.

THINGS YOU'LL NEED

Blind-building materials
like branches, leaves,
hay, plant stalks, bark . . .

SKILLS YOU'LL LEARN

Designing

Building

Experimenting

Observing

Being patient

1   Choose the place in your area where you see birds most often. This might be where birds and other wildlife feed regularly—like at a bird-feeding station, a wetland, an edge between the woods and a field, a big tree, or by a bunch of scruffy shrubs.

2   Once you find your place, get permission to build a small shelter near the site using natural materials like sticks and leaves.

3   Gather a bunch of long dead branches or look for other natural materials like old cornstalks or mowed field hay. Pile up your material like a wall in front of you, making sure it faces the area you want to watch. Make it as tall as you are when you are either lying down or sitting up.

4   Continue to camouflage it by covering it with more natural material from the area, such as dead leaves, evergreen boughs, or bark you've found on the

ground. You'll want to leave little holes and spaces uncovered so you can peek through to watch the birds.

5   Slip behind your bird blind and become invisible!

PLAY BIRD HIDE-AND-SEEK

Don't feel like building a bird blind, or maybe you don't have a spot to make one? That's okay! Look around outside and see if you can find spots that are perfect for camouflaging behind, like low shrubs, a large tree, the sidewalk side of a parked car, or the edge of a building. Think of this as playing hide-and-seek with the birds. But instead of them seeking you, you are doing it all—hiding *and* seeking.

One of my best bird-watching places in my old city, Brooklyn, New York, was a spot where I hid between two garages! No matter where you are watching birds from, the quieter and stiller you are, the more invisible you are to not only birds but other wildlife too.

HOW CLOSE CAN YOU GET?

Have you ever tried to sneak up on a bird? Try it! It's really hard to do. Even though you can't see their ears because they are tucked behind their feathers, birds have sensitive hearing, and they are always watching. Take this challenge and see how close you can get.

THINGS YOU'LL NEED

Ninja-like moves

Field journal

Pencils

SKILLS YOU'LL LEARN

Moving quietly

Spying

Observing

Describing

Sketching

1   Find a bird that's hopping on the ground. Good candidates include robins, pigeons, and other small birds. Don't try this on birds like geese or gulls because they will often defend themselves.

2   Watch the bird for a few minutes to see what it is up to. Is it searching for food, cleaning its feathers, or taking a dust bath?

3   Then, get down low—lie on your belly if you'd like—and begin to move ever so quietly and slowly toward the bird, stopping and freezing whenever it turns your way.

4   Can you get so close that you can see the color of its feet or the way its feathers overlap one another? Or hear it fluff its feathers or open its bill? Or see it breathe?

5   After the bird flies off, find another bird to try this with and see if you can beat your own record. What is the closest you can get? Record your sneaky experiences in your field journal. Draw and write about what you noticed when you were close to a bird.

ATTEND THE EARLY BIRD CONCERT

Are you a morning person? Even if you are not, set your alarm and get up to listen to a spectacular chorus at dawn. It will be worth it! Each morning in the spring through early fall, from before sunrise to a few hours after, open your window or step outside and let your ears follow the lively songs and trills of feisty singing birds. It's the male birds you're hearing, singing to attract a mate and claim and defend a nesting territory.

No matter where you live, all you need to do is listen. You've probably heard the saying "The early bird gets the worm." Well, the early riser hears the bird that catches the worm!

THINGS YOU'LL NEED

Field journal

Pencils

SKILLS YOU'LL LEARN

Listening

Tuning in

Describing

Identifying

Comparing sounds

1   Set your alarm for 1 hour before sunrise if you want, but don't worry: the chorus is most lively and loud right before sunrise, but you can still hear the dawn chorus once the sun is up.

2   Open your window or head outside.

3   Quiet your body and try some deep listening. This is a time to really focus on what your ears can hear. Closing your eyes and staying still will help. You can also try cupping your hands behind your ears. Doing this is like making the sound-catching part of your ears bigger, helping you capture more sound waves.

4   As you listen, turn your head slowly to follow the bird calls. How many different calls can you hear? See if you can hear songs from the tops of trees and other songs from the low bushes.

5   The dawn chorus is busy. Challenge yourself and see if you can pick out one song to focus on. Follow it with your ears. Does the song rise and fall, repeat itself, stop and start? What do you notice about the song?

6   Use your field journal to record what you are hearing. Don't worry about knowing the names of the birds you are hearing. Instead, write down what human words or sounds the bird songs remind you of. This will help you become familiar with individual bird songs and help you recognize them the next time you hear them. You can even try drawing a symbol of what the song sounds like to you.

Make a sound map of the bird songs and other sounds you hear. In the middle of your paper, draw a symbol to represent yourself. It could be simply an *X* or your face—you choose how you want to represent yourself on the map. Then for each song you hear, come up with a symbol for the sound and mark it on your map.

Why do male birds sing in the morning? For one thing, the early morning hours are very quiet. Other animal noises, like the chirping of crickets, have quieted down, and there is usually less wind and other natural or human noise in the wee hours of morning. So, when birds sing during this quiet time, their voices sound louder and carry farther. Also, by starting early and sounding loud, a male bird shows the female birds just how fit and strong he may be. Some dawn singers, like the American robin, don't even need to stop singing to breathe. They can breathe and sing at the same time.

DID SOMEONE SAY FREE LUNCH?

What seed-eating bird can resist sunflower seeds, corn, or a pine cone slathered with nut butter and rolled in birdseed? Setting up a fly-through, all-you-can-eat buffet is one way to guarantee that you will see birds. Try this in the winter, when there are fewer naturally available foods for birds. Feeding the birds not only gives you a chance to observe them but also to help them. You don't even need any fancy feeders—here are a few DIY ideas to turn your backyard, balcony, or window into a free lunch for the birds.

THINGS YOU'LL NEED

Toilet paper tubes or paper towel rolls

Peanut butter, almond butter, cashew butter, or sunflower seed butter

Birdseed

String, if you plan to hang your feeder

SKILLS YOU'LL LEARN

Planning

Making

Creating

Experimenting

Observing

1   Take a paper tube and spread nut or seed butter of your choice all over the outside of it. Roll your sticky tube in a bowl of birdseed.

2   Either loop a piece of string through the tube to make a hanger for it or slip it onto a tree branch. Scout around your home for the best place to feed the birds. If you have a nearby tree, hang your feeder on it. But if you don't have a tree, there are still many ways to put up your feeder. Try suction-cupping it to a window or hanging it on a hook outside. Plan to put your feeder where you can watch it from inside your home.

3   Get creative by stringing a bunch of paper-tube feeders together to make a chain or tying them to make a ladder of feeders. Be inventive where you put them too. Maybe you want to find a branch with a fork at the top and slip two feeders on the fork.

4   Be patient. It may take the birds a while to discover there is a new free-lunch spot in town.

BE A TOP CHEF FOR THE BIRDS

Become a top chef for birds by getting creative in the kitchen. Instead of a paper tube, cover something else with sticky nut and seed butters and roll it in birdseed. Try a really stale bagel, a piece of toasted bread, an ice-cream cone, an apple, a pine cone, or a piece of cardboard cut into the shape of your choice, like a star, a heart, or even a bird! Go wild feeding the birds.

15

DON'T JUST FEED THE BIRDS

BE THE FEEDER

This activity takes bird feeding to a whole new level. Instead of putting up feeders around your backyard, you will actually *become* the feeder and have birds eating right off your hat and sometimes even out of your hand! Start this in early winter. It will take some time and a bit of patience, but it will be worth it when a nuthatch eats a seed off your hat or a chickadee nibbles a seed out of your hand. Becoming the feeder works best when you have already established a bird-feeding spot, like the place where you put your paper-tube feeder (see page 14).

THINGS YOU'LL NEED

2 pieces of wood to make a scarecrow frame

Hammer

Nails

Old long-sleeved shirt

Twine

Hay, straw, or leaves for stuffing

1 pair of old pants

Pillowcase

Waterproof marker

Wide-brimmed hat

Birdseed

SKILLS YOU'LL LEARN

Designing

Planning

Building

Inventing

Being brave

Being patient

1 Build a scarecrow that is your height. Have an adult help you make the scarecrow frame by using 2 pieces of wood about the same size and shape, nailed together like a lowercase *t*. Hammer the frame into the ground.

2   Dress your scarecrow by sliding an old long-sleeved shirt over the frame. Tie off the bottom of the sleeves with some twine and tie the bottom of the shirt around the frame. Stuff some hay, straw, or leaves into the shirt to fill in the scarecrow's body.

3   Take an old pair of pants and tie the bottoms of the legs shut with the twine. Then stuff them as you did the shirt. Loop twine around the belt loops of the pants and then up and over the shoulders, like a pair of suspenders. This will attach the pants to the rest of the scarecrow.

4   Draw a face on one side of an old pillowcase using a waterproof marker. Then make a head by filling the pillowcase with your stuffing material. Tie the head to the stake at the top of the frame.

5   Place a wide-brimmed hat on the scarecrow. Make sure it fits snugly.

6   Spread birdseed on the hat, and spread more on after the birds eat it. Make sure the hat always has birdseed on it. You want the birds to get really used to landing on the hat for seed.

7   After birds start landing there regularly, it's your chance! Stand right up against the scarecrow and put the hat on your head. Make sure there is some inviting seed spread all over it.

8   Stand very still and let the birds eat right off your hat. If you are feeling very brave, you might fill your hands with seed and raise them up near the brim of the hat—birds will sometimes eat right out of your hands. As time goes on, try lowering your hands so they're right in front of you.

HAVE THE BIRDS EATING OUT OF YOUR HANDS

My friend Phil Brown feeds chickadees, nuthatches, and tufted titmice right out of his hand. To try this, hang a feeder at about head height. Make sure the feeder is always full, and notice when birds are regularly coming to it. Once the birds have discovered your feeder and know they can depend on it, instead of filling the feeder, hold a wide bowl filled with seed by the same spot. Be patient and let them get used to feeding from the bowl while you hold it. Then just hold the birdseed with your two hands cupped together like a bowl. You'll have them eating out of your hands in no time!

PSHSST!!! A SECRET WAY TO TALK TO THE BIRDS

What if you could call wild birds in so close that you could hear their feathers rustle? To make this happen, you just have to learn to *pshsst*. *Pshsst* is a secret sound that draws in some small birds like chickadees, titmice, and nuthatches. Making this sound in an area where these birds are present actually calls them in toward you, creating a charming, up-close bird encounter.

THINGS YOU'LL NEED

Field journal

Pencils

Camera (optional)

SKILLS YOU'LL LEARN

Speaking a new language

Communicating with the birds

Being patient

Spying

Observing

1   Before you do this, practice making the *pshsst* sound. It sounds just like it reads: *pshsst*. Use your normal voice to make the sound. It should sound a bit like a tire losing air. Once you've practiced a few times, you are ready to head outside and try it.

2   Outside, listen for the repeating *chick-a-dee-dee-dee* call of the chickadee. Look for them too, in the branches of trees or tucked into shrubs and bushes. This little bird has a black cap, bib, and beak; white cheeks; a gray back and wings; and a light sandy-colored belly.

3   When you hear them calling or see them flitting about, crouch down and be still.

4   Then make the *pshsst pshsst* sound in a soft voice, just above a whisper.

5   Repeat the call several times and then stop. Look and listen for the flutters and calls of chickadees and companion birds like nuthatches and titmice.

6   Repeat this calling and waiting about 8 to 10 times. If the birds are interested, they will fly to branches all around you. If you don't see or hear any response, move on and try again.

7   Once the birds have responded by flying in and landing on the trees and bushes around you, stop making the sound and just look. Use your field journal to draw a quick sketch or write down what you see. If you have a camera, try snapping a few photos of your close encounter. Don't forget to listen to what they are saying back to you!

8   After the birds have flown off, do not repeat again in the same spot for at least a few hours. The birds need to return to their regular daily activities and needs, like eating and being on the lookout for predators.

WHAT PSHSST MEANS TO THE BIRDS

Why does *pshssting* work? *Ornithologists*, scientists who study birds, aren't sure, but one theory is that the hoarse hissing sound resembles what's called a "scolding call." Little forest birds, like chickadees, sound the alarm when a predator is in the area. This scolding call tells the predator, "You've been spotted," taking away the element of surprise. It also warns other birds in the area that there's danger about. The birds gather near one another and make a riot of noise. Sometimes they even flock together to mob and chase away the predator.

Even though each type of bird has its own singing language, they often recognize the alarm calls of other types of birds. Research shows that even other animals in the forest can understand birds' scolding call. Chipmunks and squirrels sometimes even add their own chatter to the forest's emergency alert system. You, too, can learn how to recognize birds' alarm calls. This can give you a peek into the hidden world of predator and prey. If you hear the harsh scolding call of a chickadee, look around—maybe an owl is watching you!

GO ON AN OWL PROWL

Nothing says nighttime quite like the distant hoot of an owl. But did you know that you can sometimes call to them and they will call back? And sometimes they'll even fly in close to check you out! Owls will call back if they think you are another owl. That means your owl call has to be pretty good. Learning how to go owling takes practice, knowledge about the owls in your region, a bit of luck, and a lot of patience. But when it works, you'll never forget it.

THINGS YOU'LL NEED

Information about what owls live in your region and what type of habitat they prefer

Your owl call—this can be your voice or a homemade owl caller (see "Make Your Own Owl Caller" on page 21)

SKILLS YOU'LL LEARN

Researching

Learning a new bird language

Practicing

Being outside at night

Being quiet

1 First become familiar with the owls that live in your region. A great online resource to find out about owls and all things birds is the Cornell Lab of Ornithology at www.birds.cornell.edu. This site is filled with bird descriptions, range maps, photos, and a vast audio library of bird calls and songs.

2 Once you've figured out which owl species live in your area, listen closely to their calls and see if you can get your voice to mimic them. Some owls will be easier to copy than others. The great horned owl, which can be found across the entire United States, has a wonderfully deep and soft call that can be easy to imitate. It sounds like it's saying, "Who's awake? Me too."

3 When you feel ready with your call, head out on a dry, calm night with little wind. Use the information you read about the owl to choose a good location. Wait until after sunset to go and give a hoot.

4 After you've called, don't forget to listen—really listen. A great way to listen deeply is to cup your hands behind your ears to help capture the sound. Being very quiet is also important.

5   If you don't hear an owl, don't be too disappointed—owls are great at staying hidden. Try a few more times. Remember, just because they didn't call back doesn't mean they are not nearby watching you.

6   If an owl does call back, how exciting! Return its call. It may fly closer to check you out. But please remember to not go out every night to do this. Owls need to spend their time hunting, caring for their young during nesting season, and paying attention to the world around them. Calling them often might take them away from doing the things they need to survive.

MAKE YOUR OWN OWL CALLER

Learning how to call an owl with your voice is very exciting but can be really hard. An owl caller can help you. Once you make this caller, practice blowing into it to get the most realistic owl sounds.

THINGS YOU'LL NEED

Screwdriver

Empty 8-ounce soda can

Duct tape

String

Paper, crayons, and tape for decorations (optional)

1   Using the screwdriver, poke a dime-sized hole in the soda can about a half inch up from the bottom.

2   Duct tape the top of the can, covering the drinking hole.

3   Make a handy way to carry your owl caller by standing the can up and taping a length of string long enough to go over your head to each side of the can.

4   Decorate the caller by taping a colored piece of paper or drawing around the can. Make sure it's only about half the length of the can; you don't want to cover the dime-sized hole.

5   Learning how to talk like an owl on your caller will take some practice. Blow into the dime-sized hole like you're blowing into a flute. Rest the bottom of the can under your bottom lip with the hole pointing up. Blow gently down across the hole. Do not put your lips over the hole or place your fingers in the hole.

HOOT!

BE BOLD AND DIG INTO OWL BARF

Did you know that you can unlock the mystery of an owl's food chain by dissecting its barf? A few hours after an owl eats, it coughs up a pellet. The pellet, which is kind of like puke, is made up of the things the owl's body couldn't digest, like fur, exoskeletons (skeletons on the outside of animals' bodies), feathers, scales, and especially bones. By dissecting and then working to identify the bones, you can be a barf detective and figure out who was its last meal. Be daring and dissect an owl pellet today!

Don't worry if you don't have a mountain of owl pellets in your backyard. You don't even need to live near any owls to do this project. Instead, order owl pellets online. A great place to get them from is www.pelletsinc.com. These pellets are sterilized. Dissecting a sterilized pellet is safer than taking apart pellets found outside, which can carry dangerous pathogens and bacteria. Those have been cooked out of sterilized pellets, so they can be handled safely. I recommend ordering the large barn-owl pellets since they are always packed with a variety of exciting finds.

THINGS YOU'LL NEED

- Sterilized barn-owl pellet from a pellet-supply company
- Large paper plate
- Toothpicks
- Tweezers (optional)
- Rubber gloves
- Magnifying lens (optional)

- Owl-pellet dissection chart (available for free online; www.superteacherworksheets.com/owls/owl-pellet-bone-id.pdf)
- Field journal
- Pencils
- Dark paper (optional)
- All-purpose glue (optional)

SKILLS YOU'LL LEARN

Dissecting

Observing

Sorting

·
·
·
·
·

Labeling

Being brave enough to
touch owl barf

1   Once your pellet arrives, get your barf laboratory ready. Your paper plate will
be your lab table and your toothpicks will be your dissection tools. Often your
pellet order will come with a chart on bones found in barn-owl pellets, but if
not, you can easily find one free online. Don't forget to wear rubber gloves.
After all, you are dissecting barf.

2   Sterilized pellets will come wrapped in foil. Unwrap the pellet and carefully
break it in half with your gloved hands. Then use the toothpicks to pick away
the fur, feathers, or skin, searching for as many bones as you can find.

3   Sort into piles the bones that look alike to you and use an owl pellet bone
identification chart to help you figure out what kinds of animals the owl ate
before hurling up the pellet.

HOOT!

4   Use your field journal to
record your discoveries
by sketching and labeling
them. Can you rebuild an
entire skeleton from the
one pellet you dissected?
You can even glue the
bones onto a piece of
dark paper in groups of
bones that are alike or as
a complete reassembled
skeleton. Or you could get
creative and glue them in
a design, like the shape of
an owl or your name.

NEST

EGGS

BIRD POOP

BIRD CLEANING FEATHERS

FLYING BIRD

SCAVENGER HUNT: BIRDS

No matter where you live, you will always be able to find birds and signs of birds. They can lift your spirits with their songs, show you how to fluff your feathers, and remind you how to soar. Once you start noticing the birds around you, you will never be bored or alone. Keep your sharp eyes open and your ears tuned in to see if you can find everything on this bird scavenger hunt:

* LISTEN! HOW MANY DIFFERENT BIRD SONGS CAN YOU HEAR?

* LOOK! CAN YOU FIND A FLYING BIRD?

* SPY A PLACE WHERE A BIRD COULD BUILD A NEST.

* SEARCH FOR A BIRD SITTING ON A BRANCH, IN THE WATER, ON A HOUSE . . .

* WATCH A BIRD TIDY UP ITS FEATHERS.

* SNEAK UP ON A BIRD. HOW CLOSE CAN YOU GET?

* BEHOLD, IS THAT BIRD POOP? HOW MANY DIFFERENT TYPES CAN YOU FIND?

* FIND 5 THINGS YOU THINK A BIRD WOULD EAT.

* PSHSST AND SEE WHO YOU CAN CALL.

* FIND A PLACE A BIRD COULD TAKE SHELTER FROM A STORM.

MAMMALS

FUR, PAWS, AND TEETH

ACTIVITIES

Hey, it's us. We are members of the mammal club! With our warm blood, hair, backbones, and ability to make milk for our babies, we are like jaguars, river otters, chipmunks, and even the great whales. Shake your hair, look at your own paws, and chomp your teeth. We can see a little bit of ourselves every time we encounter one of our wild mammalian kin. There is still so much to discover about our own furry tribe.

Walk in the paw prints of our untamed cousins and get in touch with your own wild side by learning the ancient art of animal tracking. Find out which mammals are living in your neighborhood, conduct a squirrel investigation, follow your nose like a coyote, and unlock the food chain by learning to read the secrets revealed in poop.

GET YOUR GOODALL ON

Finding mammals in the wild isn't as easy as spying birds or investigating insects. Many wild mammals are more active at night and can be quite secretive. So, start with the mammals that live with you or around you: dogs and cats or even your brother, sister, or parent! Even though we don't often think of ourselves as animals, there is still a bit of wildness that lurks inside us and the other mammals we live with.

Get your field journal ready and become an *ethologist*—that is, a scientist who studies animal behavior, like Jane Goodall, a famous chimpanzee expert and conservationist.

THINGS YOU'LL NEED	SKILLS YOU'LL LEARN
Field journal	Observing
Pencil	Mapping
Watch	Recording
	Timekeeping
	Camouflaging

1   Pick the mammal you are going to study and find a place to observe them, like your home, a park, your neighborhood, a playground, or even a dog park.

2   The goal here is for you to watch your subject but for them not to be paying attention to you. If they focus on you, you might not see them doing the things they normally do. Try to blend into the background when you are observing your mammal by being quiet, still, and maybe even a little bit sneaky.

3   Name your subject. You can base the name on a physical characteristic. This will be handy if you watch your mammal interact with others. If you are observing a member of your family, think of a new name for them that reflects their behavior or something that stands out to you about their appearance, like Burper or Bed-Head.

4 Use your field journal to take notes on the behaviors you observe. Draw a map of their movements and consider using a watch to see how much time your mammal spends eating, being active, resting, and interacting with other mammals.

5 Take notice of facial expressions, body language, and vocalizations. How does your mammal let others know what they need or feel?

6 Observe at different times of the day. Does your mammal's behavior change?

GO DEEP WITH GOODALL

Jane Goodall's work with chimpanzees in Tanzania, Africa, was groundbreaking. Just by watching a troop of chimps over an extended period of time, she was able to observe behaviors that no other scientist had ever recorded. Find out more about her by reading one of her many books or watching documentaries about her. Or look on the internet for interviews and short videos about her work. See what you can learn from her for your work as an animal observer. Think about what wild animals you might like to spend a lifetime following and getting to know. What discoveries would you like to make?

GO NUTS FOR SQUIRRELS

We see them almost everywhere. They raid bird feeders, scamper through parks, and scurry across roads. Squirrels are so common that it can be easy to forget they are even there. But squirrels are just as feral as mountain lions or weasels. Studying squirrels is a convenient way to learn from wild mammals. Figure out what foods squirrels like best while getting a close-up chance to observe these feisty rodents.

THINGS YOU'LL NEED

1 piece of scrap wood or cardboard big enough to hold 2 cups of food in separate piles

Squirrel food choices such as sunflower seeds, birdseed mix, cracked corn, peanuts, apples, acorns, pine cones, other natural nuts, and the like

Field journal

Pencil

Binoculars or homemade tube binoculars

Watch

Wildlife camera (optional)

SKILLS YOU'LL LEARN

Investigating

Experimenting

Predicting

Describing

Recording

1 Scout your neighborhood for signs of squirrels. Look for them around bird feeders, oak trees, and other nut trees. Parks with trees are great places to focus your search. You don't even need to see squirrels to know they're around. Broken-open nut shells are usually the best clue that one or more squirrels are nearby.

2 Which foods do you think squirrels in your area like best? Nuts, seeds, fruits, and vegetables are good places to start. Pick one food you think they will like and one food you think they won't like as much. Keep the experiment simple

and healthy for the squirrels, offering only food choices that a squirrel might find in the natural habitat or at a bird-feeding station. For example, choose sunflower seeds versus apples rather than pizza versus chocolate.

3   Use a piece of scrap wood or a square of cardboard to make a feeding board. Measure out 1 cup of each food item and put it on the board, making sure that each food choice is in its own little pile. Place it in the spot where you found the most squirrel evidence.

4   Use your field journal to sketch and label your experiment setup. Don't forget to record the date and time of your experiment. Predict which food you think the squirrels will eat first and explain why you think that.

5   Tuck yourself into a hidden spot, like behind a bush or bench, to observe. Use your binoculars or homemade tube binoculars to get a focused view.

6   As you watch the food board, record the time when you first notice any animal eating from the board, but especially any squirrels.

7   Describe which food they eat first. Do you notice they are eating more of one than the other? This is their preference! Describe in your journal what is happening at the board.

8   Ask yourself: Was your prediction correct? Why do you think they like one food over another? Are they eating the food right there or taking it away? What other things do you notice? How many squirrels visit the board at the same time? What other questions can you come up with to ask yourself about this experiment?

Note: If you can't stick around to watch, don't worry. Just come back in a few hours or the next day and record what is left on the board. Did they eat all of one food and leave the other half-eaten? You can even set up a remote wildlife camera to capture the feeding action on the board! This experiment can be repeated using different foods too.

TAP INTO YOUR INNER CAVEPERSON

Humans must have been pretty good trackers to have survived as hunters and gatherers. We are hardwired to notice animal signs. We're out of practice, however. Once we let ourselves slow down, pay attention, and notice, we can become aware of the wild animals all around us. Tracking is a great way to peek into the secret lives of mammals, revealing who your wild neighbors are and what they are up to. Get your caveperson on!

THINGS YOU'LL NEED

Field journal

Pencils

Camera (optional)

Ruler

Field guide to animal tracks

Plastic bags

SKILLS YOU'LL LEARN

Tracking

Observing

Measuring

Comparing

Identifying

1   Search your neighborhood for the best tracking areas. These are the spots where an animal's paw will leave a track: sand, mud, snow, dirt, dust, and dry pavement near wet areas like a puddle.

2   Scout these places often. Remember, wild animals move a lot as they search for food, water, and shelter. If you don't find any tracks one day, you may find some another day.

3   When you do find a track, look at it carefully. Details are important. Can you tell from the print if the animal has toes? How many? Or might they have hooves? Claws? What shape is the track? What direction is it moving? Use your field journal to sketch the track and take notes on it. Photographing is also a great way to record it.

4   Use your ruler to measure the width and length of the print; also, measure the length between the tracks. Record the numbers in your field journal. Tracking field guides provide these. Can you identify the animal by using your field guide?

5   Follow the tracks! Try not to step on them as you go. You wouldn't want to wreck your find. Can you figure out what the animal was doing, where it was going, and how it was behaving? If you can, spend the day following the track. When you walk in the footsteps of another, it gives you a chance to see the world from their point of view.

6   Touch the track. feel the actual indentation where a wild animal walked. When you touch it, perhaps a little bit of the animal's wildness is touching you back.

7   Search the ends of twigs and grasses to find nibbled tips, and let your eyes wander along the ground for packed-down areas, holes in the ground, and chewed-up seeds and nuts. Using your plastic bags, pick up some of these things and start an animal evidence collection.

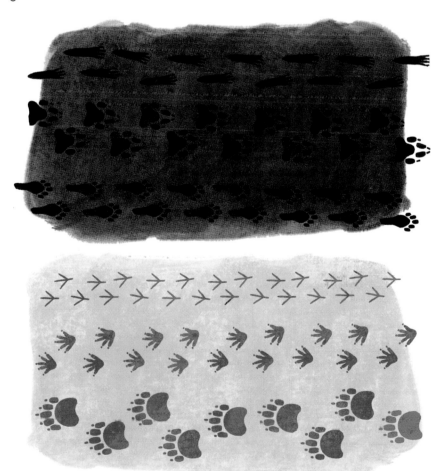

TINY TOE TUBES

Under your feet there is a whole world of small mammals. Little mice, voles, shrews, and moles are the backbone of many food webs, but we rarely see them. Wouldn't you like to know who's under your feet? By setting up a tracking tube, you can capture the footprints of these small but mighty important animals.

THINGS YOU'LL NEED

White paper

Scissors

PVC pipe, 2 inches wide x 12 inches long

Charcoal, either a chunk or a pencil

1 teaspoon nut butter like almond, peanut, or sunflower seed butter

Uncooked rolled oats

Unsalted and raw seeds like pumpkin or sunflower

Double-sided tape

Rubber gloves

SKILLS YOU'LL LEARN

Designing

Planning

Observing

Identifying

Comparing

1   Cut a piece of paper to fit inside the PVC tube and line the bottom of it.

2   Rub your charcoal on the paper. You want the paper to have a layer of dusty charcoal all over it.

3   Mix a teaspoon of nut butter with a dash of uncooked oats and a sprinkle of unsalted raw seeds, like sunflower and pumpkin. Roll the mixture into a ball and place it in the center of the charcoaled paper. This tasty bait will draw small mammals into the tube!

4   Slide the prepared sheet of paper with the bait into the PVC pipe and use double-sided tape at both ends of the paper to secure it to the pipe.

5   Find a spot for your tracking tube that is sheltered, like under some low bushes, in a tangle of tall grasses, under a thicket of brambles, by a log, or tucked next to a stump. If you have a few inches of snow, lay the tube in the snow, covering the top of the tube with snow but leaving the ends exposed. Leave it out for several nights. Many of these small mammals are most active at night and will need time to discover the tube.

6   Every few days, check the paper for footprints. The loose charcoal will show the animals' prints as they entered the tube to eat the nut-butter lure. Wear rubber gloves when handling the used paper and bait. The gloves will protect you from touching any poop that might be left on the paper.

7   Use a field guide to mammal tracks to figure out what small mammals entered your tube. That will let you know some of the ones living in your area.

SET A TRACK TRAP

What if you could bring animal tracks to you instead of having to go out and search for them? You can—by setting up a flour trap! All you need is a bag of flour and some especially good bait, like apples covered with nut butter and seeds. This is something I did regularly in the corner of my backyard growing up in Brooklyn, New York. Usually I found squirrel, mice, and stray dog and cat tracks, and I often saw blue jays and chickadees visiting the apple. On a few occasions, I even discovered opossum tracks!

THINGS YOU'LL NEED

1 apple

Knife

Nut butter like peanut, almond, or sunflower seed

Birdseed

Flour sifter

One 5-pound bag of flour

SKILLS YOU'LL LEARN

Designing

Planning

Investigating

Observing

Tracking

1   Check the weather forecast for the next few days—you will want a run of dry, not-too-windy days for this project.

2   Have a grown-up cut an apple in half. You can eat a half or save it for a snack later. They should take the other half and remove the core with a knife to make a little hollow tunnel inside the apple.

3   Fill the hollow with nut butter and spread the butter across the apple.

4   Drop birdseed onto the sticky nut-buttered apple.

5   Place the apple on a stump, a cut log, or a low rock. You want the apple raised off the ground about a foot or two.

6   Using a flour sifter, sprinkle flour on the ground around the lure. You want a thin layer of flour all around the lure as though it snowed the night before. Leave it overnight.

7   Check in the morning for footprints and nibbles on the apple bait. Continue to watch throughout the daytime for visitors like birds and squirrels. Take notes and record what you find.

WHO WILL TAKE THE BAIT?

Try different types of bait in your flour trap. The apple-and-nut-butter lure is great for enticing small mammals like squirrels, mice, and chipmunks, as well as some interested larger ones like woodchucks and porcupines. Cans of sardines are often used as predator lures by scientists studying carnivore populations. Sardines are appealing to animals such as bobcats, coyotes, raccoons, skunks, and animals in the weasel family, like ermine, mink, and even fisher.

BE A BITE DETECTIVE

Just like you, wild mammals have to eat. Each time they eat, they always leave evidence. It might be the feathers of a bird they ate, a hole they dug to get to some tasty bugs, or some scattered bits of a pine cone.

By being a sharp observer, you can learn to recognize the bite and chew marks of different animals. A great place to start is with acorns and pine cones. Over one hundred different types of animals—many are mammals—include these high-protein foods in their diet.

THINGS YOU'LL NEED

Acorns or pine cones

Magnifying lens

Field journal

Pencils

Field guide to animal signs

Plastic bags or empty glass jars

SKILLS YOU'LL LEARN

Observing

Sleuthing

Comparing

Labeling

Identifying

1   Search for acorns and pine cones. Look on the ground around trees.

2   Once you find a spot with acorns and pine cones on the ground, hunt for acorns that have been opened and pine cones that have been pulled apart. Can you find any crumbs—bits of half-eaten acorns or the leftover bits of seeds from the pine cones? Collect what you find.

3   Choose one piece to examine closely. For an acorn, use a magnifying lens to look along the edges of the acorn's shell. For a pine cone, explore the center stem and each individual scale. Can you see any tiny teeth marks? Is the acorn shell nibbled from the top down? Does the pine cone look like it was peeled like a banana? Use your field journal to sketch your observations. Label your sketch by drawing arrows pointing at the things you notice and writing down a description of what you see.

4   Since different animals have their own methods for getting at these nuts, you can use a field guide to animal signs to try to identify who ate the nuts. Once you think you've identified the eater, put the evidence in a plastic bag or a glass jar and label it with the date, location of the find, and the suspected animal.

5   Find another acorn or pine cone to investigate. Can you find one that was opened differently? This might have been done by another animal. See how many different animals you can identify just by seeing how they ate an acorn or a pine cone. Animals you might expect to identify include mice, squirrels, porcupines, deer, black bears, jays, woodpeckers, and wild turkeys.

Nuts like acorns and pine nuts are an essential food source for wildlife. Both are high in protein and calories and rich in vitamins and minerals. But did you know that they also make good people food? If you have ever eaten pesto on your pasta, you likely have actually eaten something made with pine nuts. Most store-bought pesto is made with pine nuts from trees in Europe and Asia. But people have been eating pine nuts long before pesto became popular.

Both acorns and pine nuts were important to the diet of indigenous people in places where oaks and pine trees grew. Acorns were often collected, boiled, shelled, dried, and then pounded down into flour used to make many types of breads, like tortillas and flatbreads. Charred acorns have been found in many prehistoric firepits, suggesting that they were often eaten by our ancient ancestors. (Warning: raw acorns should never be eaten and can be toxic!) Pine nuts, too, have been harvested by humans since prehistoric times. Today we eat them roasted, in soups, on top of fish and poultry, dipped in honey, in cookies, and even in a sweet pine nut brittle.

SEARCH FOR GLOWING EYES

Many wild mammals spend the day sleeping and are active at night, meaning they're mostly *nocturnal*. If you want to see them, you've got to be brave enough to venture out at night. Bring along your flashlight and shine it into a field or forest and you might be lucky enough to see a pair of glowing eyes looking right back at you. Don't freak out! These glowing eyes don't belong to ghosts. What you are seeing is called *eyeshine*—when animals' eyes appear to glow when a flashlight's beam hits them. Different mammals have different colored eyeshine. For instance, your pet dog's is red, and a bobcat's is amber. See whose glowing eyes you can find on a night walk in your neighborhood.

THINGS YOU'LL NEED

Strong flashlight

Flashlight with a red lens or red-light setting *or* red plastic wrap or red tissue paper, scissors to cut it to fit around the lens, and a rubber band to hold it on the lens

SKILLS YOU'LL LEARN

Being outside at night

Preparing equipment

Searching

Being brave

Being quiet

1   Choose your eyeshine light. This should be a powerful flashlight that you will use to scan the fields, forest edges, park borders, and wetlands for glowing eyes.

2   Pick another flashlight that you will use for safely walking in the dark. If you use a regular bright white light, the nocturnal animals will see you coming and disappear before you see them. Turn yourself invisible by using a red one. Most wild mammals do not see red light, so it will help you see them but they won't see you. Lots of flashlights come with a red-light setting or a screw-on red lens. But if yours doesn't, you can make a red covering for your light by cutting out a circle of red plastic wrap or tissue paper that is big enough to cover your flashlight lens; you can secure it there with a rubber band.

A TAPESTRY OF LIGHT

Behind the eye of many nocturnal mammals there is a special membrane called the *tapetum lucidum*, which is the key to eyeshine. The *tapetum lucidum*, meaning "tapestry of light" in Latin, has a reflective surface. When the small rays of light found in the night, like starlight or moonlight, enter the eye, they actually bounce off the membrane, giving the eye a second chance to use the light. For animals that have this additional behind-the-eye membrane, it is like having a built-in flashlight that lights a path from the inside out. What if humans had built-in flashlights behind their eyes? Imagine being able to see in the dark guided by your star-powered eyeshine! But since humans are not nocturnal, this is one superpower we don't have.

3   Wait until just after dark and head out with a grown-up. They might get scared, so be sure to explain to them that the glowing eyes don't belong to monsters.

4   Using your red-light flashlight, walk as quietly as you can. Take it slow as you walk, lifting your feet off the ground so you aren't shuffling the leaves or grass as you go.

5   Once you are away from your home a bit and near some interesting habitat for wild animals—a big meadow, the quiet parts of a park, the edge between a forest and meadow, or the shoreline of a wetland—stop and be very still for a few minutes. Listen carefully. Can you hear any noises in the landscape? Your red light won't be that bright, but it will help you see if there are any shadows out in front of you. Take some deep breaths. Do you smell anything musky or wild nearby?

6   Flick on your bright white light and search the beam of light for any glowing eyes. Scan the light across the land, low and high. If you see a pair of glowing eyes staring at you, notice what color they are and think about whether the animal you are seeing is tall or small.

7   You will have to be a quick observer. Usually once you turn your bright light on, the animal will be startled and run away from the light.

8   On your way home, discuss with your partner what animals you think you saw based on the eyeshine color; the animal's shape, size, and behavior; and any other clues you managed to find.

FOLLOW YOUR NOSE

Imagine if instead of seeing your world, you smelled your world. Your nose would tell you where to go, what was safe, where to find your friends, and even how they were feeling. For many mammals, and even other animals like insects and sharks, it's this hyperability to smell that they depend on to make sense of their world. Wolves and bears rank pretty high for having highly developed senses of smell, but did you know that guinea pigs do too? Put your schnoz to the test and see if you can follow a scent trail.

THINGS YOU'LL NEED

6-foot piece of yarn or string

Small empty plastic container with a lid

Baking extract of your choice (peppermint, vanilla, banana, lemon, strawberry . . .)

A partner

Blindfold

SKILLS YOU'LL LEARN

Following your nose

Imagining

Trusting your partner

Laying out a trail

Experiencing your surroundings the way other animals do

1   Take your 6-foot piece of yarn and put it in a small empty plastic container.

2   Cover the yarn with a baking extract of your choice. Make sure the entire yarn is soaked in the extract.

3   Let it soak for a half hour or more. While it's soaking, find a partner to help you with the next steps.

4   Take the container outside and find a spot that you won't mind crawling around on. Grass, sand, pavement, and dirt will all work well. You can even do this on snow. Just make sure that wherever you do it, you are outside, because the next steps are very messy and smelly.

5   Remove the yarn from the container. It will be drippy, wet, and soaked in the scent-filled extract, so be careful! Lay the yarn on the ground.

6   Your partner will follow the trail first, so blindfold them or have them cover their eyes.

7   Lay out a scent trail by taking the yarn and stretching it out on the ground. Make the trail challenging by having it twist, bend, or zigzag. Be creative and sneaky.

8   Lead your blindfolded partner to the start of the trail. Help them bend down and find the beginning of the yarn. See if they can follow the trail by sniffing. Remind them not to use their hands to feel the yarn or to press their nose directly to the yarn. Can they make it to the end? How did it feel for them to follow a trail just by their nose? What animal did they imagine they were as they followed their nose?

9   Then switch roles and have your partner lay out the trail for you. You'll become the sniffer with a new trail to follow.

TAKE THE ONION TRAIL CHALLENGE

Warning: this is for advanced sniffers! Don't stop following your nose after mastering the yarn trail. Take it to a whole new level by following an oniony scent trail left on trees. For this you will need at least one partner, but a whole group is even better. You will also need an onion cut in half. Divide into two groups—one group will be the trail makers and the other group the sniffers. The sniffers will close their eyes and count to 120 twice, slowly and loudly. While they count, the trail makers will take their onion half and start leaving a scent trail by rubbing the onion on trees, boulders, poles, or any other large unmovable objects. They should leave about 20 steps between each object they mark. Once they hear the sniffers getting close to the end of their second 120-count, the trail makers will need to find a final object to mark with onion scent that they can hide behind. Then the sniffers will begin the hard work of following the onion trail to find the trail makers. You can play this in the daylight, but if you really want to stretch your sniffing abilities, dusk, or even dark, makes this experience truly wild.

POW! IT'S THE POWER OF POOP

Nothing is more interesting to me as a naturalist than an animal's poop. Think of all the things you can learn from just finding a pile of this stuff—what an animal's been eating, where it went, who left it, and how long ago it was left behind. Naturalists, like me, call this stuff "scat." I like to remind myself of a little ditty I learned from a *scatologist*—that is, of course, a scientist who studies animal poop: *If you really want to know what an animal eats, take a good hard look at what it excretes!* That is why one of my most prized nature collections is not seashells, rocks, or even antlers and bones but my scat collection. Be brave, be bold, and start your very own scat collection!

THINGS YOU'LL NEED

Ruler

Camera (optional)

Field journal (optional)

Pencils (optional)

Plastic bags

Newspaper (optional)

Tape (optional)

Glass jar with lid (optional)

Field guide to animal signs

SKILLS YOU'LL LEARN

Investigating

Measuring

Collecting

Identifying

Comparing

1   Hunt for scat. Every time you head out, keep your eyes peeled for the stuff. It can be all sizes and shapes, and you can find it anywhere: right on the ground in front of you, on top of a rock, at the entrance of a den, or at the base of a tree. Avoid collecting dog or cat poop since they are too common for your collection. You can recognize these tamed pets' scat because it is usually brownish in color, looks all the same throughout, and is found where people walk their dogs or close to homes where cats might live. Boring!

2   Look at the scat with the eye of an eagle, sharp and focused, and see what you notice. Does it have hair and bones in it? Are there seeds and stems? Does it look like it's made up of shredded wood? Do you think the scat is from a predator? A plant eater? How about the shape: Is it twisty, a pellet, or a loose messy pile? And finally, where did you find it? Is it in the center of a trail, hidden and covered in the dirt, near the edge of a wetland? In a forest? A meadow? Near a house? All these things are important and will help you learn to recognize similar scat in the future.

3   Measure it. Hold your ruler near the scat, but do not touch the scat with your ruler. You want to get an idea of how long and wide it is. This will be helpful when you try to identify it.

4   And now you can collect it. Take a picture of it or sketch it in your field journal. Either is a fabulous way to document your finding. It is your proof that you found it, and it will be helpful when you look at a field guide to identify it. Include the ruler in the photograph or the measurements in the sketch. That way you will always know how big it is.

5   Identify it. There are incredible field guides to scat available to help you sleuth out who left you a number two. A favorite guide with the most comprehensive scat section is the wildlife ecologist Mark Elbroch's *Mammal Tracks and Sign: A Guide to North American Species*. Also, don't think about just mammal scat. You can search and find droppings from a whole bunch of other animals—reptiles, insects, and birds. Remember, it is really true that everyone poops! Happy hunting!

Warning: When you find scat, do not use sticks to break it apart. This would wreck the shape, which is key to identifying what animal left it. More importantly, when you break poop apart, it can release very dangerous bacteria and pathogens into the air that you could inhale.

GLOWING EYES

NUTS

ANIMAL POOP

PINE CONE

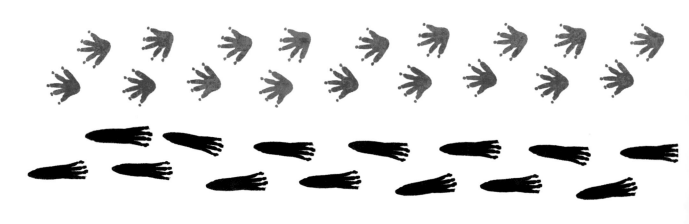

ANIMAL TRACKS

SCAVENGER HUNT: MAMMALS

Wild mammals are hard to find. Many of them are really good at avoiding humans by sleeping during the day, camouflaging, and having super senses that help alert them to our presence. Yet if you are really paying attention, you can find clues of their existence every day. See what you can find on this mammal scavenger hunt:

* A CHEWED NUT OR PINE CONE

* THE TRACK OR TRAIL OF A MAMMAL

* A PLACE WHERE A MAMMAL COULD HIDE FROM YOU

* SOMETHING A MAMMAL WOULD WANT TO SMELL

* EVIDENCE OF FEEDING

* MAMMALS COMMUNICATING

* SOMETHING A MAMMAL PREDATOR WOULD EAT

* WILD ANIMAL POOP

* EYESHINE

* THE ENTRANCE TO A BURROW OR DEN

47

HERPS

THAT'S AMPHIBIANS AND REPTILES TO YOU!

ACTIVITIES

Have you ever wanted to catch a frog? Make a home for a toad? Search for snakes in your own backyard? Are you ready to explore a group of animals that can be as small as your pinkie fingernail or as big as a school bus? If you answered yes to any of these questions, then you are ready to get into *herping*—that's the search for and study of an amazing and diverse group of animals: amphibians and reptiles.

PUT THIS IN YOUR BACKPACK

When you are out herping, you don't need much equipment, but there are a few important things you'll need to know before you head out. For your safety, begin by reading up on what kinds of snakes you are most likely to find in your community. Since some snakes are venomous and can be life-threateningly dangerous, taking the time to research them will help you stay safe. Learning to recognize the snakes in your region that pose a risk to your well-being is the only way to do this.

And for the safety of the amphibians and reptiles you find on your exploration, head out on this trip with your rubber gloves on. Since some of these creatures breathe through their skin, wearing rubber gloves, like a scientist or doctor, will protect the animals from breathing in any bug spray, sunscreen, lotions, soaps, or even salt that might be on your hands.

ROLL A LOG/LIFT A ROCK

Tucked under rotting logs and rocks, a whole world waits for you. These dark and hidden hideaways are perfect spots to begin your search for salamanders, frogs, toads, and snakes. You might even be surprised by what else you will find in these undercover homes! Let's explore this secret world.

THINGS YOU'LL NEED	SKILLS YOU'LL LEARN
Rubber gloves	Searching
Magnifying lens	Observing
Field journal	Identifying
Pencil	Mapping
Camera (optional)	Being brave

1   Find a place that has rotting logs or rocks you can lift up. If you don't have those nearby, look for a spot where there are flowerpots or garbage cans on the ground.

2   Get ready to be a superfast observer. Once you lift a log, roll a rock, or tilt up a flowerpot, whatever has been hanging out under cover will scurry or slither away from the light. To warm up your seeing skills, take a few moments to squat down low, be still, and see how many animals you can spy with your eyes or hear with your ears. Tune in to the wild world around you.

3   Then, kneeling by the log, rock, pot, or can, roll or lift it away from you. If it is too big to move, find another one. Sometimes the smallest, rottenest log has the best finds.

4   Quick! Look underneath for animals or signs of animals. Search for the silvery trail of a snail or slug, ant tunnels and ant larvae, earthworm burrows, small mammal holes and their cache of seeds and nuts, spiders and their webs, burrowing beetles and insect larvae, snakes or their shed skin, salamanders, toads, and small frogs.

5   If you find a hidden herp, don't feel like you need to catch it. Instead, watch it and observe its reaction. If you want to catch one of these animals, remember to put on your gloves. If you are handling a snake, of course, make sure it's not a venomous one. Hold the animal down low near the ground so that if it escapes from your hand, it won't fall too far. After a few moments, let it go back where you found it.

6   Use a magnifying lens to look at this microhabitat. Even if you don't see any amphibians or reptiles, it doesn't mean they weren't there at one point. What can you find that a snake would eat? Where would a small salamander hide itself in this dark world? Are there any lizard footprints? If you were a small wood frog, would you be able to survive here? Write notes in your field journal.

7   If you have a camera, snap a photo to capture the scene. If you don't, use your field journal to make a quick map of your finds.

8   When you are done looking, carefully put the object back in place, gently, making sure not to let it fall hard back into its spot. With the rock, flowerpot, or garbage can, place it back almost on the same spot but not exactly. This way, nothing is pressing down on any animals left in the space.

SEARCH FOR SNAKE SKIN

Imagine if, when you grew, you actually grew entirely out of your own skin and left it behind when your new, bigger skin was ready. Many herps do exactly this. They shed their skin as they grow or when it becomes too tattered and worn. Snakes are masters at slipping out of their own skin. They begin by rubbing their snout against something rough, like a rock, tree bark, or sand. This helps them tear a hole in their old skin so they can slither out in their new covering. If you have ever found a snakeskin in the wild, it is usually inside out. It's just like when you pull off your socks.

You can look for snakes' shed skin in woodpiles and rock walls and along rocky ledges. Once, while searching for frogs, I watched a northern water snake shed its skin underwater. It was in the gravelly part of a pond, and I watched as it rubbed and squirmed, slipping off its old, tattered coat. When it was finished and its fresh scales glistened in the sunlight, I collected its old skin from the water, dried it out, and still have it today!

CROAK IT, OR HOW TO HEAR THE LOVE SONGS OF FROGS

Birds aren't the only animals that sing to attract a mate. Every spring and summer, down along the freshwater wetlands of our world, countless male frogs stake out territories and let their love songs rip! On warm nights, you can hear the high, squeaky chirps of tiny spring peepers and the deep, low croaking of mighty bullfrogs. So, grab your flashlight, pull on some rubber boots, and head to the nearest wetland with a friend—you won't want to miss your chance to listen to the wild frog chorus!

THINGS YOU'LL NEED

Field journal

Pencils

Rubber boots or shoes you don't mind getting wet

Flashlight with red lens

Cell phone that can record sound (optional)

SKILLS YOU'LL LEARN

Recognizing frog calls

Identifying

Being quiet

Listening

Being outside at night

1   Choose a night to go on a listening search with a grown-up. Either walk or drive very slowly around your neighborhood with your car windows open. Listen for peeps, trills, croaks, and ribbits. When you think you hear some frogs calling, record the location in your field journal. You will need to make sure you can safely walk down to the spot and that it isn't on private property. Great places to listen for frogs are at nature preserves, parks, and town beaches with freshwater wetlands.

2   The next warm night, head with your grown-up to the spot you found with the most frog calls. This time, put on your rubber boots or old sneakers that can get wet and bring a flashlight with you. If you have a cell phone, you might want to bring that too, so you can record the frog calls.

3   As you walk toward the frog chorus, tread slowly and as quietly as possible. Frogs are incredibly sensitive to sound and will stop singing if they hear you coming. Use your flashlight to help light your way. Remember, you can go invisible by using your red lens (see "Search for Glowing Eyes" on page 40).

4   The closer you get, the more likely the frogs have sensed your arrival, so turn off your light and be patient, quiet, and still. They will eventually start calling again. When they do, let the sound wash over you and take it all in. How many different types of calls can you hear? Are they calling from the wetland's edge or are they out in the middle of the water? How do you think they are making the sound? What do the sounds remind you of? How many frogs are calling?

5   Turn your light back on and scan the perimeter of the area. Can you see any of the singers? Even though a frog chorus sounds like there are frogs all around you, they can be really hard to spot. When you see them, watch closely to see how they are making the call. You might notice that it looks like they are blowing their necks out, almost like a bubble. Their song is made by the air from their lungs vibrating their vocal cords and then the stretchy neck pouch expands and amplifies the sound, like a loudspeaker!

6   If you can, record the sound on a cell phone using the voice memo app or by taking a video. By collecting the sound this way, you can listen to it again at home to see if you can identify all the different types of frogs chorusing.

7   Come back to the same wetland throughout spring and summer to listen to the frog chorus. It will change as different frogs finish their mating season and new species start their singing.

Tip: If you aren't sure what to listen for, check out the nature recordist Lang Elliott's webpage at https://musicofnature.com/calls-of-frogs-and-toads-of-the-northeast/, where you can listen to the different frog calls most often heard in North America and see photos of the frogs that make these amazing sounds.

BECOME A FROG WATCHER

Be a helper to scientists—just by listening to frogs! Consider putting your frog listening skills to use by joining in the Association of Zoos and Aquariums' FrogWatch USA citizen science program. You'll help scientists collect data on frog populations, diversity, and species accounts. All you need to do is listen for frogs and toads from early spring through late summer and then submit your finds to a national online database. To find out how you can become a frog watcher, visit FrogWatch USA at www.aza.org/frogwatch?locale=en.

PEEP! PEEP! PEEP!

RIBBIT!

BE A HERP HERO

Birds and bugs are all around, and even wild mammals that we see less often leave footprints and scat around for us to find. But amphibians and reptiles go almost unseen by us. Though they live all over the world—from mountaintops to oceans and cities to country swamps—most people don't know they are there. You can be a herp hero by finding them, documenting their existence, and letting your state's wildlife agency or area conservation group know about them. Knowing which amphibians and reptiles live in what places can help protect these species.

THINGS YOU'LL NEED	SKILLS YOU'LL LEARN
Field guides to your region's amphibians and reptiles	Researching
Field journal	Identifying
Pencils	Surveying
Camera	Mapping
	Documenting

1   Research which amphibians and reptiles are found in your region. Field guides and online searches will help you come up with a list.

2   Make your own field guide in your journal. Include sketches or photographs and notes on the habitats of each species from your list that you're going to search for. Make sure you know if there are any venomous snakes on your list and exactly what they look like.

3   Choose a nearby habitat to search. Make sure you have a camera for your outing. You will need to take photos of the species you find to document them. Be sure to search on a warm day. All amphibians and reptiles are cold-blooded, which means their body temperature is determined by the temperature of the air or water that surrounds them. The colder the temperature, the less active they'll be, and they will stay in a protected place where they can rest, making it hard to find them. But when temperatures are between 60 and 80 degrees Fahrenheit, get your game on and go!

4   Lift and look under logs and rocks, and always remember to put everything back as you found it. Search sunny spots, too, for basking lizards, snakes, and turtles. If you can, check out the edges and shorelines of different types of wetlands, from swamps and marshes to rivers and lakes. Be a super-quiet searcher. Some of the herps you seek are alert not only to sound but also to vibrations. So, no stomping, please!

5   When you find a herp, be quick with your camera and snap some photos. You will need photos to send to your state's wildlife agency or area conservation group.

6   In your journal, record the species you found, where and when you found it, and what it was doing. Create a map to show its location. This can come in handy if you want to search for it again. Imagine if you found a rare species! Having a map will help you show the scientists where to locate it. Even if you have already found an amphibian or reptile on your list and you find it again, photograph and record it again. Seeing a lot of the same species is as important as seeing it just once. It can help prove that a certain habitat is important to protect.

7   When you get home, send your photos along with your checklist notes to your state's wildlife agency or area conservation group.

SEEK AND YOU WILL FIND

Identifying animals in nature can be hard. There are so many details you have to look at—from colors and shapes to size and patterns. Before you head out to search for the amphibians and reptiles of your area, you might want to sharpen your identification skills first. You can do this by making "trading cards" for each animal. Like a Pokémon or sports card, your herp card can include a picture of the amphibian or reptile and a few bulleted points about its *field marks*—its features that can help you tell it apart from similar animals. If you like, you can even make a set of cards for all the wild animals you find in your backyard. It will help you become familiar with how to recognize the wild creatures around you.

Field guides are a great resource to help you learn how to recognize animals that you find, but sometimes you don't have your field guide handy. If you have access to a cell phone, you can use the Seek app, which was developed by iNaturalist. All you need to do is use a phone to snap a picture of your find and then Seek will provide you with an identification. Your photo needs to be clear and detailed so the Seek app can make the best match possible.

SALAMANDER

CATCH A FROG BARE-HANDED

Can you imagine holding a wild animal in your hands? Looking at it eye to eye while feeling the gentle pulse of its life? Setting it down and watching it hop off to live the rest of its life in the wild? Well, you can! Kids have been catching frogs for hundreds of years. We know a lot more about these amphibians now than in olden days, and frogs, like many animals now, need our help and care more than ever. You really don't need to catch a frog to have an eye-to-eye encounter. You can admire it by being a super observer. You might even see it catch a fly or defend its territory from another frog. But if you really need to catch a frog, here are five easy steps to help you have an encounter with a frog that is safe for the frog and good for your soul.

THINGS YOU'LL NEED

Rubber boots or shoes you
don't mind getting wet

Rubber gloves

SKILLS YOU'LL LEARN

Handling a wild animal

Showing compassion

Being gentle

Being quick

Demonstrating grit

1   Go to a wetland where you have seen frogs before and search the edge of the area for these long-legged jumpers. You might see them floating in the water or sitting along the shore.

2   When you see one you think you can reach, put on your rubber gloves, sneak toward it, and then crouch down low. Slowly, quietly, carefully raise your hand over the frog's back from behind. In one quick motion, reach toward the middle of the frog's back. Grasp the frog in your hand with your thumb under its belly and your other fingers gently wrapped around the body, right behind the front legs. Catching a frog is hard. They are slippery and have lightning-fast reflexes, so you might not catch it the first few times you try. When you catch one, don't squeeze it. Instead, hold your hand loosely around the frog and squat down in case it jumps free. And never hold a frog by its back legs, as that's dangerous to the frog.

3   While it's in your hand, stay curious about how it feels and what it looks like up close. Take only a few moments to hold the frog. Being held by a big human giant is not the frog's idea of fun. It stresses them out, so be kind and let the frog free soon after you catch it. Even though it might be tempting to catch it again, don't. Find a new frog to watch instead!

DIY FROG NET

You don't have to catch a frog with your bare hands. Instead, you could use a fishnet that you can buy from wherever fishing equipment is sold. I like to use a telescoping pond net, used by wetland scientists around the world. Its handle can extend for those frogs that are too far away to reach. But you can also make your own net by following these simple directions:

THINGS YOU'LL NEED

Bug net	Pliers (optional)
Duct tape	Fishing line
Metal hanger	Bamboo cane or long stick

1   Get a bug net bag from a garden supply store or purchase one online. These are inexpensive bags made out of a mesh that you slip over plants to protect them from insects, but they also make a perfect net for frog catching!

2   Take a metal hanger and, using your hands or pliers, straighten the hook. Then bend your hanger into a rounded shape. You want to make sure the bug net bag is big enough to go around the hanger frame. You might have to adjust the size of the frame to fit your net.

3   Use fishing line to sew the bug net bag onto the hanger frame by doubling the bag around the frame.

4   Put the hanger's straightened end into a bamboo cane or long stick from a freshly cut sapling and tape securely using waterproof tape.

BUILD TOAD HALL

Invite a toad to your backyard by building a home for it! Toads are actually a type of frog, but unlike other frogs, who have slimy, slippery skin and often live near or in water, toads have dry, bumpy skin and can be found wandering around gardens, forests, and edges of fields. Having a toad live near you will give you a chance to watch this fascinating amphibian make its living in your backyard.

THINGS YOU'LL NEED

Hand shovel

Old flowerpot or large tin can
(like a coffee can)

Decorations of your choice (optional)

Field journal

Pencils

SKILLS YOU'LL LEARN

Designing

Building

Observing over time

Mapping

Recording

1   Find a place a toad would like to call home. Scout your backyard, front yard, local park, or community garden for a shady spot. If it is going to be in a park or at a community garden, make sure to ask for permission first. The best time to build a toad a home is from early summer through late summer.

2   Using a hand shovel, dig out a spot for the flowerpot or tin can so it can be buried halfway when placed on its side.

3   Decide if you want to decorate the toad home. You can use waterproof, nontoxic paints or markers, or you can go all out and use natural materials, like little stones, tiles, and bark that you glue onto the pot or can. You only need to decorate half of it, since the other half will be buried in the ground.

4   Lay your toad home on its side in the hole you dug and bury it so only half of it is showing.

5   Place a few handfuls of dead leaves inside the can and a few small rocks near the entrance. These last few finishing touches will help the toad feel more at home by providing it with a sense of being hidden and protected.

6   Draw a map to the toad home in your field journal including any nearby spots that you think a toad would find inviting, like a nearby garden, rotten log, shady moss, or a compost pile.

7   Check your toad home regularly for a toady resident. If you find one peeking back at you, make it feel welcome by quietly observing it. Use your field journal to record its behavior. Be curious about what a toad does during the day. When does it seem most active? Does it seem bigger each time you see it? Is it there every time you visit? If not, where is it and what do you think it's doing?

8   If after a few weeks a toad hasn't moved in, try a new spot. Ask people in the area if they have ever seen a toad in the neighborhood. If you don't have toads in your area, still set up your toad house outside. Maybe another animal will move in, like a lizard or salamander.

SNIFF LIKE A SNAKE

Watch a snake and you will think it's sticking its tongue out at you over and over. It isn't being rude; it's just giving you a sniff. A snake sniffs with its tongue, collecting odor particles from the air. These bits of smelly air molecules are then sent to a special pair of organs found on the roof of the snake's mouth. The Jacobson's organ, also known as the vomeronasal organ, relays the smells to the snake's brain. The snake then knows whether to slither away because of danger or to go after its prey. How do you think your tongue would do at smelling the world around you?

THINGS YOU'LL NEED

Several smelly spices

A partner

Blindfold (like a bandana or a knitted hat you can pull down over your eyes and nose)

Small plate

SKILLS YOU'LL LEARN

Smelling with your taste buds

Imagining

Trusting your partner

Experimenting

Experiencing your surroundings the way other animals do

1   Look in the spice drawer at your house and choose a few smelly spices like garlic, pepper, cinnamon, or chili powder.

2   Cover your partner's eyes and nose with a bandana or even a knitted hat that you can pull all the way over their nose. Make sure they can still breathe but that they can't see and that their nostrils are covered.

3   Pour a little sample of one of the spices you've chosen onto a small plate.

4   Have your partner stick out their tongue. Ask them to roll up their tongue like a straw if they can. Bring the plate toward their tongue, but do not let their tongue touch the spice.

5   Tell your partner to breathe in through their tongue and mouth. Ask them if they can "smell" the spice just from pulling in the air and its spicy molecules through their tongue and mouth. See if they can name the spice or describe the spice they are sniffing.

6   Now you try!

TONGUE POWER

Snakes aren't the only reptiles that use their tongues to smell—lizards do too. But, then, why do snakes and lizards also have nostrils? They need them to breathe, just like us, but most scientists agree that their nostrils don't do much sniffing. That's all up to the tongue—and for all snakes and a few lizards, this means having a forked tongue. Being able to "sniff" the air with a split tongue helps these reptiles pinpoint the direction of the odor they are finding. Snakes don't just use their sniffy tongues to find dinner or escape from being someone else's meal; they can also follow scent trails left by other snakes to their winter dens or even to find a mate. Next time you see a snake or lizard flick its tongue at you, flick yours back and see if you can smell it!

MAKE A HERP AT HOME

Want to make an inviting spot for frogs, toads, salamanders, snakes, and lizards? All you need to do is set up a *cover board*, a small piece of untreated wood, about the size of a picture book, laid on the ground in a shady, moist spot. Scientists use this simple shelter to help conduct studies on amphibians, reptiles, and other animals. See who you can invite into your own cover board.

THINGS YOU'LL NEED

Scraps of wood from picture-book size to bigger and as thick or thicker than a quarter inch

Field journal

Pencils

Camera (optional)

SKILLS YOU'LL LEARN

Setting up an experiment

Observing

Mapping

Describing

Sketching

1   Choose an area that is somewhat damp and shady and a bit out of the way, so other people don't find your cover board and turn it over too early or get rid of it.

2   In spring, summer, and early fall while the weather is still warm, gather your picture-book-sized pieces of scrap wood—a few is all you'll need—and lay these boards directly on the ground.

3   In your field journal, draw a map of where you placed your boards and the date you laid them out. Predict what animals you think you will find under your boards and what you think it will look like under the cover boards after a month has passed.

4   Wait at least a month before you flip your boards over and see who has taken shelter.

5   Be ready to observe. Once the boards are flipped over, the animals that were taking shelter under the boards will want to get out of the light as soon as possible. Use a camera to capture what you see or make quick sketches in your field journal. Draw a map of what you see under the board, including where any amphibians, reptiles, or other creatures are found. Think about how the cover boards changed the habitat from when you first put them down.

6   When you are all done looking at all your cover board finds, place the boards lightly on top of the original spot and visit them again a few weeks later. Notice if your discoveries change through the season. Keep mapping the little world under the boards. Does it look different? Are there always the same animals? Do you see new tunnels or excavations? How does this microhabitat change over time?

7   When you are done with your cover board experiment, remember to take your boards back home. You can use them again in a new spot.

SEARCH FOR HERP HIDEOUTS

A cover board works because animals take shelter under the board just like they would under a log or rock. Setting up a few of these sanctuaries around your neighborhood is a great way to find out who is hiding under the surface. Try different types of cover boards—corrugated tin, ceramic tiles, log rounds, or even an old towel—to see if they attract different types of animals. Experiment with the spots you choose to place the boards. Damp and shady areas might attract different herps and animals than dry, sandy locations.

Also, look around your area and see if you can find any natural places that would offer herps refuge from predators and the weather. Reptiles need a place to shelter when the weather is too cold for them to move, and they also need a place to keep cool during the hottest days. Using your field journal, make a map of where you find these resting nooks, and check them frequently during the summer season for any sightings of amphibians and reptiles. Remember to look for the shed skin of snakes and some lizards. You can also search for tracks, like the track of a slithering snake or the drag marks left by a turtle's shell.

WRANGLE A SNAKE LIKE A PRO

My friend Matt Patterson has been watching, touching, and catching snakes, frogs, and turtles since before he could walk. He doesn't even remember a time that he didn't love these animals. Growing up in New Hampshire, he's had his chance to spend time with all kinds of snakes, like the small, slender ring-necked snake and the bold northern water snake. Now an award-winning wildlife artist and reptile and amphibian conservationist, he still spends his days and nights searching for, observing, and sometimes catching all types of reptiles and amphibians. Matt is a pro snake wrangler, but his favorite way to be with a wild snake is to watch it. He says, "That's when you see the good stuff, like how it moves or hunts. That's when you can really get to know it." If you want to catch a snake, though, here are Matt Patterson's snake wrangling tips for beginners.

THINGS YOU'LL NEED

An experienced snake wrangler to partner with you

Snake stick

SKILLS YOU'LL LEARN

Recognizing local snakes

Handling nonvenomous snakes

Showing compassion

Being gentle

Being brave

1   "Don't try this alone," says Matt. Go snake searching with someone who has caught snakes before and knows how to identify the local snakes, especially if you live in a place with venomous snakes. You don't want to make a rookie mistake. It could be dangerous to your own safety, and if you don't handle the snake carefully, you might end up injuring it. If you don't know anyone who is into snakes, see if your region has a herpetological club that you can join, or reach out to a nearby zoo or nature center to help you find a fellow snake charmer.

2   Study up on your local snakes and start with the small, easygoing ones. One of Matt's favorite snakes to share with beginners is the ring-necked snake. This petite snake, when caught, will rarely try to bite, and if it does, its mouth is often too small to get a hold of you.

3   When searching for snakes, walk quietly and slowly. Snakes are very sensitive to vibration and sound. When you find one, first make sure you know exactly what kind of snake it is, so you'll have a good idea of its behavior. Avoid catching snakes with aggressive behaviors, like the northern water snake, and do not try to catch any venomous ones.

4   Use a snake stick (see "Make Your Own Snake Stick" to find out how to make one) by placing the Y end behind the snake's head. Then slowly and gently grasp the snake right behind the stick, close to the back of the head. Gently lift up its head while your other hand supports the rest of its body. Do not just hold it by its neck. Snakes need to have their whole body supported or they can be injured.

5   Stay low to the ground in case it slithers right out of your hand. The calmer you are, the calmer the snake will be. Let your hands be relaxed, not squeezing the animal.

6   Be prepared for the "smelly sauce," as Matt calls it. This is when snakes let loose a stinky, poop-like musk all over you in hopes of you being so disgusted that you'll just let it go. The smelly sauce has a truly foul aroma, a stench described as a mix between rotting eggs and dead fish. Even though each snake has its own particular stinky-sauce odor, they all pretty much reek! Don't let this stench stop you. Matt always thinks of it as part of the snake-catching experience.

7   Let the snake slide through your hands and just visit with it for a few moments, then let it go. It has places to go and food to find! To free your serpent, place it down on the ground, near where you found it, letting its body go first and then its head.

MAKE YOUR OWN SNAKE STICK

In third grade, Matt made a tool that has been helping him catch snakes even to this day—a snake stick. This special stick holds the snake behind its head so you can pick it up without worrying about the snake turning its head to bite you. It is easy to make and will help keep you and the snake safe from harm. All you need is a straight stick about 1 foot long with a branching Y at the end. Matt made his by cutting a sapling down to size and trimming the end with the Y so each branch is about 2 inches long. He carved off the bark and then he even carved a snake's head into the other end and painted it to look like a real snake! What kind of snake will you make your stick look like?

GO ON A BASKING HUNT

Since reptiles are cold-blooded, an important feature of their habitat is having a place to bask. Basking is when they lie in the sunlight, raising their internal body temperature so they can be active in their environment. It's a bit like when you get out of cold water after swimming and you sit in the sun to warm up. Basking is also important to reptiles because it keeps them healthy by enabling their bodies to take in important vitamins and minerals, and it keeps their skin—and in the case of turtles, their shells—healthy. If you can figure out the good basking spots in your area, then you've got it made. You will know exactly where to look for these hard-to-find wild creatures.

THINGS YOU'LL NEED	SKILLS YOU'LL LEARN
Binoculars	Observing
Field journal	Mapping
Pencils	Recording
Outside thermometer (optional)	Temperature taking and reading
Camera (optional)	Spying

1   Have you ever sat on a stone and almost burned your buns off? Or stepped on hot rocks and sand at the beach and felt like your feet were on fire? When you are looking for basking stops, think of these kinds of hot, rocky spots. Search for where rocks and sunlight meet, such as mountain ledges; the edges of ponds, lakes, and other wetlands; and in deserts, fields, and meadows. Along the edge of wetlands, on hot summer days, you can often spy snakes and turtles basking in the sun, with some of their body still staying cool in the water, just like you might, on a hot summer day, have your toes dipped in a pond while you sit on the beach.

2   Scan these spots with binoculars on warm mornings in the late spring, summer, and early autumn. If you see a lizard, snake, or turtle, slowly and quietly approach. Remember that they are always on high alert for sound or movement, so try your best to move like you are invisible.

3   Once you've found a basking site, chances are you will see it being used again and again. It is even possible to find turtle, lizard, and snake poop at these spots, so you might consider taking a photo to document it. (See "Pow! It's the Power of Poop" on page 44.)

4   Set up a basking watch by hanging out near the site with your binoculars and field journal. Record what you see. Is the reptile facing the sun? Are its eyes open? Does it seem to stretch itself across the whole site? How long does it bask? Is the site being used by more than one animal? If so, document the behavior you see between animals.

5   Bring an outside thermometer with you and see what the temperature is at your watching spot. If you can get near the basking site when it isn't being used, take the temperature on the site. Is it different than where you were sitting? If so, by how many degrees? Can you feel the temperature difference with your hand?

6   Look around the site. Can you find the sheltered place where the snake or lizard might go when it gets too hot? If you are watching a turtle, look into the water. Where would it need to go to hide if a predator came? Make a map of the basking site in your field journal and show where you think the reptile goes when it isn't basking.

ALL ABOUT BASKING

Reptiles aren't the only animals that bask. From meerkats and butterflies to vultures and sea lions, many different types of animals are regular sunbathers. Some, like reptiles, are cold-blooded and need the sun to help warm up their internal temperature so they can become active. This is also true for insects like butterflies and dragonflies. Watch for them perching on plants in the morning sunshine. See how they spread out their wings like catchers' mitts, collecting the sunlight to help warm their whole body.

SUN

TOAD

SNAKE

LOG

SCAVENGER HUNT: HERPS

You are now on your way to becoming a *herpetologist*—that's a scientist who studies amphibians and reptiles. These animals need some superstars to help people understand their important role in the natural world. Herps are an essential part of the food webs of the world, eating bugs and rodents and being eaten by hawks, owls, and other important predators. Here's your chance to help the people in your neighborhood understand not only the importance of these animals but also how incredibly amazing they are. On this scavenger hunt, invite someone who you think could learn to love herps along with you. See if you and your partner can find:

* A ROTTING LOG THAT WOULD BE A GOOD SALAMANDER HOME

* A SUNNY SPOT WHERE A SNAKE WOULD BASK OR SHED ITS SKIN

* THE NEXT BEST PLACE TO MAKE A TOAD HOME

* SOMETHING THAT YOU CAN SMELL BY BREATHING IN THROUGH YOUR TONGUE

* A SPOT A TURTLE MIGHT CALL ITS HOME

OTHER THINGS TO TRY:

* TELL YOUR PARTNER SOMETHING SPECIAL ABOUT A HERP THAT LIVES IN YOUR REGION.

* MAKE THE SOUND OF A FROG FROM YOUR STATE.

* CATCH AND RELEASE ONE FROG OR SALAMANDER.

* MOVE LIKE A SNAKE, HOP LIKE A FROG, AND CRAWL LIKE A SALAMANDER.

* PRACTICE CATCHING A SNAKE BY USING YOUR SNAKE STICK ON A BIG WORM.

ARTHROPODS

INSECTS, SPIDERS, AND MORE

ACTIVITIES

Do you want to get face-to-face with a wild animal? Look no further than the arthropods—that's insects, spiders, crustaceans, and more! There are more arthropods on Earth than any other animal. With well over a million different species, having a hands-on, up-close encounter with at least a few of these amazing animals every day is easy as pie.

From insects to spiders and crabs to millipedes, members of this tribe all have segmented body parts, legs made up of more than one joint, and an exoskeleton, which means their skeletons are on the outside of their bodies—not inside, like ours. They also have stunning superpowers. Can you shoot silk out of your arms like a spider or make your belly glow in the dark like a firefly or unhinge your bottom jaw like a dragonfly nymph? Be brave and explore this astounding group of animals. You can find them anywhere on this Earth, even inside your own home! You will never feel alone if you spend time getting to know the arthropods of your world.

PUT THIS IN YOUR BACKPACK

Since many arthropods are quite small, having a magnifying lens will help you notice them in greater detail. If you don't have a lens, did you know that your binoculars can double as a magnifier? Simply flip your binos upside down and with one eye look through one of the eyepieces. If you hold something small in your hand and lower the lens to it, the upside-down binos will work as a decent magnifier. If you are using your homemade tube binoculars, they won't magnify, but they will certainly help your eye focus.

PETAL STAKEOUT, OR HOW TO SPY ON A BUNCH OF BUGS

Spend time spying on a flower and you will be amazed at all the stories that unfold. From the hungry, fuzzy bumblebee in search of nectar to the quiet, camouflaged spider waiting to capture its next meal, flowers are hot spots of arthropod activity! By staking out a blossom, you can witness arthropods eating, mating, hunting, communicating, and so much more.

THINGS YOU'LL NEED	SKILLS YOU'LL LEARN
Flowers to spy on	Spying
Magnifying lens or binoculars	Observing
Field journal	Sketching
Pencils	Describing
	Recording

1   Choose a flower in the sun that you can easily see and be close to. It can be big or small or even part of a bush.

2   Make sure you get comfortable since your stakeout could take a while. You want to be about a hand's distance away from the flower. Now just watch! If you can, get down low and see if there are any creatures hiding under the leaves or tucked beneath the petals. Let your eyes wander from the very bottom of the stem to the top of the flower. Use your magnifying lens to get a close-up look at the flower's visitors.

3   In your field journal, record who visits the flower, what they do there, and how long they stay. Sketch and describe the visitors. Are they flying to the flower or crawling on the flower? Where are they spending their time on the flower?

4   Check out other flowers in your area. Are there different animals visiting different flowers? How do you think they find the flowers they choose to visit? Where are they going after they leave? Do you notice any patterns to their visit? Try this at different times of the day and see if you get different visitors.

THE BUZZ ON BUMBLES

Have you ever spied on bumblebees? Look for these insects buzzing in and out of flowers. Bumblebees are easy to recognize because of their large size, furry bodies, short stubby wings, and loud buzzing. The loud buzzing is actually the sound of the bee vibrating as a way to shake out the pollen hidden deep in the flower. To make this buzzy sound, bumblebees unhook their flying muscles from their wings and begin to quiver intensely. This whole-body vibration shakes the pollen grains right out of the flower and onto the bee's fuzzy body.

Bumblebees have another trick to get pollen out of flowers. Their bodies have a positive electrical charge, while flowers have a negative charge. Since opposite charges attract, when a bumblebee lands on a flower, the negatively charged pollen is drawn to the positively charged furry body of the bee.

DO YOU DARE HOLD A DADDY LONGLEGS?

Have you ever noticed the very thin-legged, spiderlike animal in your yard, a park, a field, or a forest? Daddy longlegs, also called harvestmen, look like spiders but they aren't. To find out how these animals are different from spiders, read "Who's Your Daddy (Longlegs)?" on the next page.

One of my earliest animal memories is spending time with my father in my backyard in Brooklyn. Our yard wasn't very big, but there was a sliver of wildness at the hydrangea bushes. We would watch the daddy longlegs crawling along the damp, leafy ground. Resting our hands on the cool leaves, we'd wait patiently for these busy urban harvestmen to trot across the tops of our hands. I remember how it tickled me as I watched their small, button-like bodies bounce between their eight long legs. To this day, each time I encounter one of these stilt walkers, I'm brought right back to the hydrangeas and my dad in our little slice of wild backyard. Now it's your turn—dare to let a daddy longlegs wander across your hand!

THINGS YOU'LL NEED

Daddy longlegs

Magnifying lens

SKILLS YOU'LL LEARN

Handling a wild animal

Showing compassion

Being gentle

Being brave

Observing

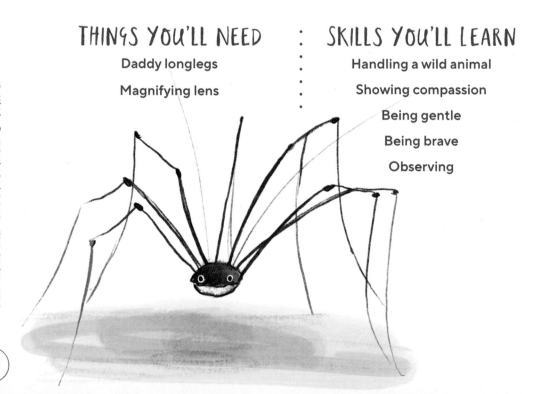

1   Search gardens, fields, bushes, and forest floors for daddy longlegs. Late spring through early fall is the best time of the year to find them.

2   When you find one, place your hand out in front of it and let it crawl aboard. Try cupping your hands around it, but be ready, because this bug is all about crawling. With its long, flexible legs, it can be very active in your hand. Remember to squat low to the ground when you are handling any animal so that if it falls out of your hand, it won't have far to fall. And be careful of its many legs—they are long, thin, and fragile. Do not hold the daddy longlegs by its legs. It needs them for not only walking but also sensing its environment.

3   Letting a daddy longlegs walk across you can tickle, and you might feel like jerking your hand away quickly, almost like a reflex. Try to take a deep breath and don't worry, they can't bite you. Their mouths are too small. If it is just too much for you, you can gently shake the bug off your hand.

4   If you notice a foul stink, that is the daddy longlegs telling you that it is stressed out. Its smelly fart is one way this animal defends itself, since it has no fangs or venom. Imagine if you could protect yourself just by cutting the cheese!

5   When your daddy longlegs visit is done, let it go where you found it. Then spend some time watching where it goes and how it moves. At the end of each of its legs is a little hook that helps it hang on to and climb plants, stems, and rocks. Can you find one that is hanging upside down on the underside of a leaf or climbing up the bark of a tree? Use your magnifying lens to get a close-up.

WHO'S YOUR DADDY (LONGLEGS)?

Daddy longlegs are arachnids like spiders, but they are not actually spiders. Although they share some similarities, like having eight legs, they are quite different. They have one body segment and two compound eyes, whereas spiders have two body segments and eight compound eyes. Compound eyes contain thousands of lens, unlike human eyes, which have only one lens. Other differences are that, unlike spiders, daddy longlegs don't produce silk and they do not have fangs or venom.

Daddy longlegs have a broad diet that includes tiny spiders, small slugs, earthworms, mites, and small dead creatures. They have even been known to eat each other! Daddy longlegs are food for birds, insects, and spiders.

SHAKE A BUSH

Tucked into the leaves and branches of bushes, shrubs, and hedges is a whole hidden world of little creatures. It might be hard to tell just from walking by a shrubby plant, but a bush can be shelter, food, and nursery to many small invertebrates. An *invertebrate* is an animal without a backbone. An easy and exciting way to see a sample of this diversity is to give the bush a shake.

THINGS YOU'LL NEED	SKILLS YOU'LL LEARN
Old, light-colored bedsheet	Observing
1 strong stick	Collecting
Magnifying lens	Comparing
Field journal	Sketching
Pencils	Describing
Camera (optional)	

1   Find a shrubby plant. That means look for a bush, hedge, thicket, or even a young, small tree. Spread out an old, light-colored bedsheet at the base of the plant.

2   By shaking the shrub firmly but gently, you'll dislodge the tiny animals inside, who will fall onto the sheet. The best way to shake the bush is to use a strong stick to rattle the leaves and branches. Start at the top of the plant and work your way down, shaking the leaves, branches, and even the trunk of the plant. Remember to be gentle. The bush you are shaking is the home, nursery, and feeding spot for many animals.

3   When you are done rattling the plant, you can use the sheet as a way to pick up a creature without having to actually touch it. If you slide your hands under the sheet and cup them under the animal you are interested in looking at, the sheet will act as a barrier between you and the animal.

4   Look carefully at the entire sheet to see the sample of animals that have been spending time in the bush. What types of bugs do you see? How many different types of bugs can you count? Use your magnifying lens to take a close-up look at a few and sketch them in your field journal.

5   When you are done looking at the animals, carefully pick up the sheet from the corners, turn it upside down over the bush, and shake the remaining bugs back onto the bush.

6   Try repeating this with different plants. Compare your finds from one plant to another. Consider shaking the same bush throughout the year. It is a great way to see change over the course of different seasons. Take a picture of the sheet each month. If you live where it is cold in the winter, you can even try this then. You might be surprised by what you can shake out of a bush in the winter.

CAN YOU FIND THE CAMO CATERPILLARS?

When you are looking at the animals you found, notice how many of them are colored to blend in to the bush they are living on. Can you find a caterpillar that looks like a twig, with its body colored brown or gray to match the branches of the bush? These sticklike caterpillars sometimes even have bumps on their bodies to help them camouflage on the rough twigs they call home. Look for these camouflage experts in the spring and summer. They will be eating the foliage of the shrub or tree where you found them, and they will eventually spin cocoons and transform into their adult stage as moths or butterflies.

THROW A MOTH PARTY

Night is a perfect time to see moths, or as my daughter calls them, "moon butterflies." Mothing is an exciting night adventure for your family to get involved in. Throw a party and invite other friends and family to join your picnic for the moths.

There are thousands of different kinds of moths and, with their velvety wings and feathery antennae, they have a beauty all their own. The butterfly gets all the attention in the day, but turn your gaze to these soft, furry insects when the sun goes down and you will not be disappointed.

You can invite moths to your backyard and neighborhood by baiting some nearby trees with a sweet concoction. The recipe calls for a bit of beer. This is for the moths, of course, not for you, so make sure your grown-ups know this. This technique is best during the spring to fall months, when the nighttime temperature is over 50 degrees. The moths are drawn to the sweet scent of the bait and will come to lap up the lure. Here's how to do it.

THINGS YOU'LL NEED

Wide-mouthed container with lid

1 overripe banana

One 12-ounce can or bottle of beer

3–6 tablespoons molasses
or brown sugar

Big paintbrush

Flashlight with red lens

Field journal

Pencils

Magnifying lens

Camera (optional)

Field guide to moths and/or
insects (optional)

SKILLS YOU'LL LEARN

Cooking for moths

Observing

Comparing

Identifying

Being outside in the dark

1   Using a wide-mouthed plastic container, mash the overripe banana with the beer and a bit of molasses or brown sugar until the mixture is pudding-like. You want it thick, not drippy. Cover the container and let it sit in the sun for a few hours or even the whole day.

2   Just before dark, paint as many trees as you can with the mixture. Use a big paintbrush to spread the bait in a 1-foot square about 3 to 4 feet off the ground. Try not to spill any of the lure on the ground or let it drip down the trees. If your mixture is drippy, go back and add more molasses to help thicken it. Drips attract ants, and they will eat the mixture before the moths can get there.

3   Wait about a half hour and then return with flashlights to check the baited trees. It is best to use a red light on your flashlight. (See "Search for Glowing Eyes" on page 40, to find out how to turn your regular flashlight into a red light!) There should be plenty of moths attracted to the sweet concoction, along with other insects.

4   Recheck the trees throughout the evening to see who else shows up for this irresistible moth treat. In your field journal, sketch and describe some of the moths you discover, or take photos. What do you notice about the variety of colors moths come in? Can you watch them closely enough to see them lap up the sticky treat with their long, curly tongues? Are there any other kinds of creatures attracted to the bait?

CELEBRATE NATIONAL MOTH WEEK

Another way to attract moths during the warm nights of spring, summer, and autumn is to hang a white sheet between two trees or even on an outside laundry line. Shine a bright light on the sheet to draw in the moths.

To help you get started looking at moths, check your region for activities on moths, especially during National Moth Week (NMW), which takes place annually the last full week of July. NMW is a worldwide celebration of the important ecological role that moths play in our world. All across the US there are events and programs during this week that can help you and your family discover the incredible beauty and diversity of these fuzzy flying creatures. Check out this website to find out more about NMW: http://nationalmothweek.org/.

MAKE YOUR OWN BUG POOTER

A bug pooter is a simple and handy tool used by *entomologists,* scientists who study insects. It's like a vacuum that lets you suck up bugs into a clear container so you can study them without hurting them. Making your own pooter and learning how to use it will really help you collect and observe insects that can be hard to catch, like flies or teeny-tiny bugs that are so small you can't pick them up with your fingers.

THINGS YOU'LL NEED

Clear and clean plastic container
with a lid

Hole puncher

Bendy straw

Scissors

Clay or putty (small amount)

1 piece of nylon from a pair of
old tights

Heavy-duty shipping tape

About 1 teaspoon uncooked rice

Magnifying lens

Field journal

Pencils

Camera (optional)

SKILLS YOU'LL LEARN

Designing

Making

Experimenting

Collecting

Observing

1   Take a clear and clean plastic container with a lid and, using a hole puncher, punch 2 holes on opposite sides of the container. Be sure to make the holes below the lip of the container so you can still put the lid on it.

2   Cut your bendy straw in half. Place the bendy half into one of the holes in the container. This straw half will be your vacuum hose to suck up bugs. Plug up the hole in the container around the straw with clay or putty so it's airtight.

3   Cut a small piece of nylon, about 2 inches wide, from an old pair of tights and fold it in half. Then tape the nylon around one end of the other straw half. Make sure to use strong tape, like the kind for sealing a package to put in the mail.

4   Push the straw with the nylon end into the other hole in the container. You might need to make the hole a little bit bigger so the nylon-wrapped straw end will fit. This is the filter end of your bug sucker. The nylon filter will stop you from sucking up any bugs into your mouth!

5   Once the straw is in, seal the hole with clay or putty to make it airtight.

6   To use your pooter, put the lid on your container and practice with some grains of rice. Sprinkle out a few grains of rice. Position the bendy straw near the rice and put the other straw in your mouth and suck in. You should be able to pull the rice into the container and hopefully not into your mouth. If you end up with a grain of rice in your mouth, something is wrong with your nylon filter. Double-check and re-tape.

7   Take your pooter on an adventure. Head outside and see what little bugs you can suck up. Once you have a bug in your container, use your magnifying lens to look at it. Spend time with the bugs you catch, observing, sketching, describing, and even photographing.

8   Once you are done looking at your catch, set it free back where you found it.

WHO IS POOS AND OTHER IMPOOTANT POINTS

Who invented the pooter? This favorite tool used by mini-beast scientists everywhere is also known as an insect aspirator. It was first used and reported on by the American entomologist William Poos in 1929. Poos's invention became widely used and his name was forever attached to this handy piece of bug-studying equipment.

GO ON A WATER BUG SAFARI

Below the water's surface is perhaps one of the best places to find a wide variety of arthropods. From caddisfly larvae and bloodworms to crabs and crayfish, you never know what your next scoop will find. Exploring from the edge of any wetland like ponds, lakes, streams, and swamps as well as tidal pools, salt marshes, and the shore of the ocean always delivers. Equipped with just a kitchen strainer and a bucket, you will not be disappointed.

THINGS YOU'LL NEED

Rubber boots or old sneakers that can get wet

Clothing that can get a bit wet or muddy

Tray or old pan

Bucket

Kitchen strainer

Ponding net (optional)

Spoons

Tweezers (optional)

Ice cube tray (optional)

Empty and clean small plastic containers (optional)

Field journal

Pencils

Variety of field guides, like those for pond-life, fish, amphibians and reptiles, and insects (optional)

Magnifying lens

SKILLS YOU'LL LEARN

Collecting

Sorting

Identifying

Comparing

Counting/inventorying

1 Choose a spot along the shoreline of any wetland that gives safe access to the water. Avoid steep banks, slippery rocks, muddy edges, and other rough, hazardous, or fragile terrain.

2 Fill a tray or an old pan and a bucket with the water from the wetland. A tray is good for looking at small invertebrates, while a bucket can be deep enough to hold larger catches, such as predacious diving beetles.

3 Dip the kitchen strainer into the water and then gently press it into the edge of the bank or the bottom of the wetland. A ponding net is also a great tool for collecting creatures. With its long handle, a net can help you reach farther out into the wetland without having to wade in. Ponding nets are available through fishing supply stores and nature/science study catalogs, or you can make your own; see "DIY Frog Net" on page 59.

4 Each dip into the water has the potential to find some creatures. Bring them up to the tray or bucket and carefully remove them with a spoon, tweezers, or even your fingers. You can also remove them by simply turning your strainer or net upside down into your collection container.

5 Take time to look at your finds. Consider sorting your catch into groups of creatures that look alike. If you are sorting small creatures, use an empty ice cube tray to make your groups or use empty and clean small plastic containers, like yogurt cups. If you want to look at a bug up close, you can also use a spoon to pick up the bug and some water. Remember, these are aquatic bugs and must stay in the water to survive.

6 Use field guides to identify the animals you have found. Keep a list of your finds in your field journal, with short descriptions and sketches of each animal. Record the total number of each type of animal you identify. Sometimes this information can shed light on how healthy the wetland is that you are exploring.

7 When you are done, return all creatures to the wetland by gently pouring your collection back into the water.

8 Thoroughly clean your equipment before you leave by dipping it into the wetland and swishing it through the water. Also, when you get home, clean it again by spraying it out with a hose and using a bit of dish soap. Once it's clean, let all your equipment dry in the sun for several hours. This will help disinfect your equipment so that the next time you use it, you won't be spreading any invasive plants, diseases, or other threats into other wetlands you explore.

DEW THE WEB

Have you ever seen a spiderweb glistening with morning dew or covered with water after rain? They can be quite beautiful and magical-looking. The spiral-patterned web is a gorgeous masterpiece and at the same time an intricately engineered meal trap for the spider. With a spray bottle in one hand and a magnifying lens in the other, let's get up close and personal with the spiders in your neighborhood.

THINGS YOU'LL NEED

Spray bottle with water

Field journal

Pencils

Camera (optional)

Magnifying lens

SKILLS YOU'LL LEARN

Investigating

Searching

Observing

Sketching

Describing

1   Head outside to search for spiderwebs with your water-filled spray bottle in hand.

2   Look for spider silk in all sorts of places, including the corners of buildings, between two weeds, on the ground, on the top of a shrub, under a leaf, and any place else you can imagine a spider might live.

3   When you find a web, use your spray bottle to gently coat the web with water. Don't soak it. Instead, just mist the web.

4   Record the web in your field journal by sketching it and describing it. If you have a camera, you can also take a photo of it. Is the web a spiral shape or more like a tangle of silk, or is it like a sheet? Where did you find it? List whether it is located on the ground or suspended off the ground. Are there any bugs caught in the web? If so, what do they look like?

5   Now search for the spider. Can you find the maker of the web? If so, what does it look like? About how big is it? What is it doing? Sometimes, if you blow on

the web, that will shake the web and the spider will crawl out to see if it has caught its next meal. When you get a chance to see a spider up close, use a magnifying lens to look at its coloration and the shape of its two body parts. This will help if you want to identify it.

SPIDER SILK'S SUPER-POWERS

Did you know that scientists and engineers have been trying to make spider silk for decades? The invention of an engineered version of spider silk material, with its ability to stretch and its stronger-than-steel reputation, could revolutionize our human world—from building materials and textiles to medical uses and cosmetics.

Spider silk is pretty fantastic stuff. It is lightweight, waterproof, superstrong, and soft, and it can stretch long distances without ripping. Made of proteins formed inside the spider, the silk starts as a liquid, hardens to a solid, and then is spun into a fiber. Many spiders can make up to seven different types of silk that are used in different ways, from building a web to wrapping up prey in a sticky trap.

Humans have been collecting and using spider silk throughout history for uses that range from making fishing lines to even bandaging wounds. This material has been a useful tool in our development. Humans aren't the only animals that have made use of spider silk. Many birds use it as a component of their nests to hold together nest materials. How would you use spider silk?

DO A BUG SWEEP

You won't need a broom to do this kind of sweeping, but you will need a long-handled bug net. If you don't have one, you can make one; see "DIY Frog Net" on page 59. If you don't have time to make a net, you can go really low-tech and use an old, thin, light-colored towel, like a kitchen towel. From spring through fall, swishing and sweeping your net or towel through grassy meadows, lawns, fields, and forest edges is like going on safari right outside your front door. You won't be catching lions or tigers, but you will be discovering a wild world of wild mini-beasts that will blow your mind!

THINGS YOU'LL NEED

Bug net or an old, light-colored towel

Variety of field guides, like those for insects, spiders, caterpillars, and butterflies

Plastic containers with lids

Magnifying lens

Field journal

Pencils

SKILLS YOU'LL LEARN

Collecting

Observing

Identifying

Sorting

Comparing

1   Grab your net or towel, some field guides, a few clear plastic containers, and your sense of adventure and head to the nearest grassy area.

2   Choose a grassy spot that has more than just one type of grass. Habitats with varieties of grasses, wildflowers, and other plant life will be home to more diverse wildlife, which means more exciting finds.

3   When you've found a good spot, use your net like a broom, sweeping it back and forth across the grass. Sweep your net from side to side, moving it from the top of the grass to the middle section and finally along the ground. If you are using a towel, follow the same motion—waving the towel across the grass.

4   As you pull in your net, cinch the top of the net closed. If you are using a towel, grab the ends to form a little sack, where hopefully your catch is waiting for you to look at it.

5   Look at your catch in the net without opening it up. You should be able to see some of the animals crawling up the side of the mesh. Check that you haven't caught any wasps, hornets, bees, or other stinging or venomous creatures. If you have, just open your net and shake it out and start again. If you are using a towel, lay your towel down on the ground and open it up. Sharpen your powers of observation because as soon as you open your towel, some of the animals you caught will fly, hop, or scurry away.

6   If you want to look at an animal more closely, take your plastic container in one hand and reach into the net with it. Use your other hand on the outside of the net to guide the creature into the container, and then slide it up to the top of the net and quickly put the cover on. If you're using a towel, simply take the plastic container and pop it over the animal you want to check out. Then slip the cover between the towel and container. Be careful not to squish the bug. Or, use your pooter!

7   Use your magnifying lens to observe your catch. Is it an insect, with its three distinctive body parts—head, thorax, and abdomen? Are you looking at an arachnid with eight legs and its usual two body parts—thorax and cephalothorax? Perhaps you've caught a juvenile form of an insect, like a caterpillar? Can you identify it using field guides or the Seek app? Record your discoveries in your field journal through sketching and describing.

8   When you are done looking at your finds, remember to set everyone free.

MAKE YOUR OWN BUG HOTEL

One of my favorite things to use when I'm looking at arthropods is my bug hotel—a cardboard box that I made into a screenhouse just for arthropods. It's like a big terrarium that I can shake my sweep net's contents into and then observe my finds. Making your own bug hotel is easy. You might need to ask for help from a grown-up since this will involve using a knife to cut cardboard.

THINGS YOU'LL NEED

- Empty cardboard box
- Duct tape
- Utility knife
- Scissors
- Window screening

1   Tape up all the sides of the box except for the opening. Then, using the utility knife, cut large windows out of the sides of the box. You only need to cut two of the sides, but if you want to get fancy, you can put windows in all four. When you are cutting the windows out, make sure to leave at least 3 inches of frame around the edge. This will help stabilize your bug hotel and give you some space for taping on the screens.

2   Using scissors, cut the screens to fit the windows of your box with enough extra screening that you can tape it securely to the frame around each window.

3   Tape the screens into the windows from inside the box. Use enough strong duct tape to make your screens tight and secure.

4   Now your bug hotel is ready to use. Remember, though, to empty out your hotel when you're finished. Bugs have places to go, food to eat, and families to make. If you keep them captive, they won't be able to survive.

SEARCH FOR YOUR WILD HOUSEMATES

Imagine going on a wildlife safari without ever leaving your home! Well, you can, and you don't even need a TV, computer, or phone screen. No—this is all about searching your home's nooks and crannies for the arthropods that already live there. Think ladybugs, stink bugs, spiders, ants, silverfish, and flies. Wherever humans live, other animals share our shelter and the crumbs we leave behind. Scientists are just beginning to pay attention to the human home as habitat. By participating in iNaturalist's Never Home Alone project, you can help researchers document what arthropods are found in your home and also find out what people from all over the world are finding as their unexpected roommates. Get ready to get wild inside!

THINGS YOU'LL NEED

Magnifying lens

Camera

Field journal

Pencils

SKILLS YOU'LL LEARN

Observing

Collecting data

Photographing wildlife

Sharing finds with scientists

Participating in citizen science

1 Search inside your home from top to bottom for signs of animals. Keep a sharp eye open for cobwebs in your corners, ladybugs in your window frames, ants in your cupboard, and little silver bugs in your drawers.

2 Each time you find an animal, use your camera to document it, and record in your field journal where you found it, what it was doing, and the date and time you found it. Use your magnifying lens to see all the fascinating details of the animal.

3 Upload your finds to the Never Home Alone website at www.inaturalist.org/projects/never-home-alone-the-wild-life-of-homes. If you can, identify the

arthropods you are uploading. You can use the photos on the site to help you figure this out. If you don't have any idea, don't worry. The scientists who manage the site will try to identify the creature.

4   Spend some time on the site exploring what types of arthropods people are finding all over the world. Think about which arthropods are the most common in people's homes and why that might be. Also, consider why scientists might be interested in finding out which bugs live in our homes. How does sharing your home with bugs make you feel? Can you think of any benefits to having bugs as your housemates?

5   Try this inside-your-home wildlife safari during different seasons. Do you find different bugs? Why or why not?

YOUR GUT, HOME TO MILLIONS

Scientists aren't only interested in the bugs that live with us—a whole new realm of study is taking off on the wildlife that lives *on* us and *in* us! Did you know that our bodies are actually self-contained ecosystems for a whole slew of microscopic living creatures?

The newest and most exciting ecosystem that scientists are studying is the microhabitat of the human gut! Recent research suggests that our health might be tied to the health of our internal ecosystem. The better habitat you have inside of you for gut microorganisms, like bacteria and fungi, the healthier you will be. How do you give your gut buddies a good place to live? Scientists and researchers aren't sure, but some evidence suggests that healthful eating, regular exercise, and a good night's sleep might be part of the key. When you take care of your body, you are also taking care of all the microscopic organisms that call you their home!

BEE

CHEWED LEAF

FLYING INSECT

ANTHILL

SCAVENGER HUNT: ARTHROPODS

Every day, no matter where you live or what you are doing, arthropods are somewhere nearby, living their fabulously different lives. What wild opportunities await you when you wake up to the arthropods of our world! Think small, search with your magnifying lens, and be bold as you seek out the incredible diversity of these animals. Can you find the following?

* A BEE COLLECTING POLLEN

* A SPIRALING SPIDERWEB

* A CHEWED LEAF

* AN ARTHROPOD INSIDE YOUR HOME

* SOMETHING A MOTH WOULD FIND DELICIOUS

* AN ANTHILL THAT YOU CAN WATCH

* A FLYING INSECT

* NOW LISTEN. HOW MANY INSECT SOUNDS CAN YOU HEAR?

* HOW MANY PREDATORS CAN YOU FIND THAT WOULD EAT A BUG?

* HOW MANY ARTHROPODS CAN YOU FIND ON A TREE?

OTHER INVERTEBRATES

WORMS, SNAILS, SLUGS, AND STARS

ACTIVITIES

What kind of animal are you if you're not a bug, bird, fish, amphibian, reptile, or mammal? Welcome to the world of worms, snails, slugs, clams, coral, stars, and a whole host of other creatures that call planet Earth their home. Imagine if you didn't have a skeleton, either inside you like humans or outside you like insects or spiders. You might be something soft and squishy like an earthworm or maybe some soft-bodied animal tucked into a fortress made of shell, like a snail or a clam.

Summon a snail, stalk a giant earthworm, make your own snail slime, and muck about with mollusks! All you need to do is roll up your sleeves, pull on a pair of boots, get down on the ground, or wander along the edge of a swamp, pond, tidal pool, or ocean edge to meet this crew of wild and diverse animals!

HOW TO HOLD A WORM

Here's your chance to hold a wild animal in your hand and not have to worry about being bitten! Worms have no teeth! The only thing they might do is squeeze out some slimy yellow liquid. Don't freak out—it's not pee. It's *coelom*, a fluid that worms release when they are stressed. So, if you get slimed with yellow goo, it means it is time to put the worm down. Okay, it might also actually poop in your hand. But don't worry. It's just like a little dot of dirt. After all, you must have heard that worms make dirt, right? Well, they do this by pooping it out! Welcome to the world of worms! Ready to become a world champion worm wrangler?

THINGS YOU'LL NEED

Spray bottle with water

Magnifying lens

Field journal

Pencils

SKILLS YOU'LL LEARN

Handling a wild animal

Observing

Showing compassion

Being gentle

Being brave

1   Find some earthworms. Look in gardens, in sidewalk cracks, under leaves, beneath garden pots, by stumps, and in rotting logs. Try looking for them right after it rains. Don't try finding them in the cold of winter, though—they'll be hibernating deep underground.

2   Have a small spray bottle filled with water handy when looking for worms, and spray your hands before you pick up a worm. Since worms breathe through their skin, having damp hands will help them be more comfortable and prevent them from drying out. You can also moisten your hands in the nearby dirt, grass, or leaves. Pick up the worm gently. They've got no bones, so their bodies are soft and squishy. Hold the worm down low to the ground so if it wiggles out of your hand, it won't have far to fall.

3   Use your magnifying lens to see the wormy details. What do you notice? Feel the worm squirm around in your hand. How does it move? Can you figure out

which end is its head? How do you think it senses the world around it? Does a worm have a top side and a bottom side? Pay attention to where it tries to go and how it behaves while being held. Record what you notice in your field journal.

4 If it releases coelom on you, take the hint. The worm is stressed. Try re-dampening your hands to make it more comfortable. If it continues to release the yellow slime, let it go where you found it.

Earthworms might not have bones, but they are all about their muscles! Did you notice the rings around its body? Watch these as the worm moves. Notice how the worm gets really long and then contracts as it inches along your hand. These rings are surrounded by muscles. Along each segment there are *setae*, which are tiny bristles that stick out of the worm's body. The muscular segments, along with the bristles and a slippery slime the worm produces, help the worm move where it needs to go. This boneless little creature is a champion at not only moving but also mixing Earth's soil.

FLEX YOUR MUSCLE, WORM

GO ON A NIGHT CRAWLER HUNT

Are you ready for the Night of the Crawler? Don't be scared—think giant worms, slimy bodies, and an outside adventure after the lights go out! Grab your flashlight with your red filter and a grown-up who doesn't mind a nocturnal quest of the wormy kind, and head outside for a night you will never forget.

THINGS YOU'LL NEED

Flashlight with a red lens
(See page 40 for how to make your own.)

SKILLS YOU'LL LEARN

Being outside at night

Observing

Spying

Worm wrangling

Being quiet

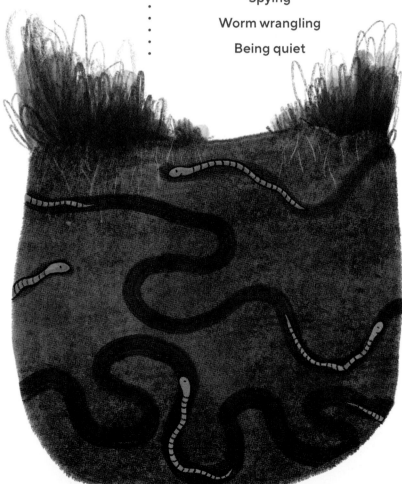

THE ANIMAL ADVENTURER'S GUIDE

1   Pick a rainy, warm night in spring, summer, or fall and go visit a garden. Vegetable gardens are the best location for this expedition.

2   As you approach, be very quiet. Walk as silently as a coyote by letting your heel down gently first and then rolling forward onto the balls of your feet. Worms can sense vibrations with their stiff and bristly setae, so the less you stomp, the better your hunt will go.

3   Listen for the strange scraping sound of these large earthworms as they slide back into their burrows when they feel you approaching. Can you believe you can hear them as their bodies rub against the soil? How would you describe the sound? Can you hear them when they come out of their burrows too? Is the sound the same or different?

4   Look for their big pinkish-tan bodies poking out of the dirt. You can also look for a silvery line in the garden bed near their holes. This is left by the mucus that covers their whole body and helps them move. Think of it as body snot.

5   If you are feeling bold, rub your hands in some dirt and try to catch one of these biggies. They will be slimy and slippery, so remember to hold them down low in case they slip out of your hand. Don't try to pull them out of their burrow. Their setae will help them grasp the sides of the hole. You might end up tearing them in half. It is not true that when worms are halved you end up with two live worms. Instead, you usually end up with an injured worm or, even worse, a dead worm.

6   Can you find a cone-like pile of little round balls next to a burrow? It's a nice, tidy mound of castings. What's casting, you ask? Well, that's worm poop. Don't worry, this poop doesn't stink. In fact, it's full of nutrients from the dead organic material that worms eat. This poop returns all the good stuff back to the earth. Way to go, worms!

BE A SLIME TRAIL DETECTIVE

Tracking a deer or fox is something most people have heard about, but did you know that you can also track a snail or slug? These two related animals don't leave footprints, but on land they do leave a different kind of trail that you can learn to recognize and follow: a slime trail! This kind of trail is actually a mucus trail—yep, like boogers. This isn't from the snail's or slug's nose, since they don't have one. Instead, it's their foot snot! This slime helps them move. Their body produces the goo and then their muscular foot slides along on it, which comes in handy for climbing and sticking to vertical surfaces. Are you ready for your first case as a slime trail detective?

THINGS YOU'LL NEED

Field journal

Pencils

SKILLS YOU'LL LEARN

Observing

Noticing

Sketching

Tracking

Sleuthing

1   From late spring to early fall, search for silvery wandering trails left on plants, dead leaves, rocks, and soil. The best time of day to search for this is in the morning before the sun dries the trails up and they disappear.

2   When you find a slime trail, follow it! You might just find the snail or slug that made it. It won't be able to scamper off like a squirrel or fly away like a blue jay. Take your time and visit with one of these amazing animals. Their ancestors left slime trails where dinosaurs once stomped the earth.

3   You might not always find animals when you track them, but you can figure out what plants they have been visiting. Many snails and slugs eat plants, and are often considered garden and flower pests. See if the slime trails lead you to a leaf, flower, or vegetable that looks like it has been eaten. Use your field journal to take notes. Draw the trail and sketch what you think has been eaten.

GET FACE-TO-FACE WITH A SNAIL OR SLUG

Get up close with a snail or slug. The best places to search for them are damp, shady spots. Sunlight and heat are dangerous to these soft-bodied animals, drying them out and even killing them. Some of my favorite spots to look for them include in rotting logs, on mushrooms, under damp leaves or bark in the forest, and in any garden at night. Rainy or damp summer mornings or early evenings are good times to go slug and snail hunting.

When you find one, you are in for a treat. Look at its head, where you will find four tentacle-like stalks. The two tall ones on top of its head are for sensing light and also for smelling. It would be like us having eye-noses. The two smaller ones lower down on its head are used for feeling and tasting. That would be like us having tongues on our fingers! All four stalks can move independently of one another and are retractable! Slugs and snails can make the stalks disappear, pulling them into their body when they feel threatened. If something happens to one, they can regrow it! Those are just a few facts about the head of these fascinating gastropods that belong to the phylum Mollucsca, the same group as octopus and oyster. What else will you discover about snails and slugs?

MAKE TIME FOR SLIME

Snails and slugs are expert slime makers. Their slime is a gooey mucus made up of water, salts, and proteins. It not only helps them move but also protects them from drying out and even from being eaten by some predators. Here's how to make your own slime so you can explore the properties of this fascinating substance.

THINGS YOU'LL NEED

8-ounce bottle nontoxic white glue

2 teaspoons baking soda

2–3 tablespoons contact lens saline solution

Mixing bowl

Measuring spoons

Mixing spoon

Field journal

Pencils

Resealable plastic bag

SKILLS YOU'LL LEARN

Making

Experimenting

Investigating

Creating a substance that mimics something in nature

Imagining

1 In a mixing bowl, combine the nontoxic white glue with the baking soda and stir until this sticky substance is well mixed and smooth.

2 Slowly add the saline solution to the mixture. Stir until it's stringy and then slowly add a little more saline solution and then a little more until the slime begins to form balls. Now you've got your own slime to explore.

3 Feel it, squish it, fold it, and stretch it! What does it feel like? How would you describe its properties? Is it a solid or a liquid? Is it hot or cold or something else? How do you think this homemade slime is like or not like real snail and slug slime? Can you find something to move through the slime that mimics a snail?

4   Scientists are trying to make copies of snail and slug slime in the lab. They have some ideas of how it might be helpful for humans. Can you think of ways this booger-like stuff could be used by people? Write down your ideas in your field journal. Maybe you will be the scientist who finds that slug slime will save the world!

5   When you are done exploring your slime, store it in a plastic bag you can seal until you are ready to get slimy again!

SLIMY CURES

Snail slime can help keep wrinkles away? Cure pimples? Soothe cuts? It is amazing to hear how people have been using this mucus through centuries and what scientists are now finding out about it. Throughout history, it has been used to treat cuts and burns. Not only was the stretchy, gooey consistency easy for coating wounds, but some snail slime is also actually antimicrobial, protecting cuts from infection, researchers have determined. The slime is now being used as an ingredient in skin care, especially in the treatment of acne and in wrinkle creams. Not only are scientists looking at slime as a pimple cure, but engineers are using slime to make new types of glues that might change how we build things, treat cuts, and even do surgery.

Not all snail and slug slime is safe, though, so don't go rubbing snails or slugs on your face or putting them on your cuts! A few can carry parasites that can be very dangerous to humans. The best advice if you get slimed is to wash your hands well with hot water and soap.

BUILD A SNAIL TRAIL ADVENTURE

Become a snail for a day and see the world from its point of view. Don't worry, you won't need to drink a strange potion or lick a snail's foot to transform. All you will need is your imagination and a bit of string. Then get down low, move slowly, and see the world up close.

THINGS YOU'LL NEED

3-foot-long piece of string or yarn

Backpack

Magnifying lens (optional)

Small sticks (optional)

Field journal

Pencils

SKILLS YOU'LL LEARN

Designing

Imagining

Observing

Mapping

Sharing

1 Bring your piece of string or yarn outside and search for an interesting tiny landscape, like a place that has rocks, stumps, or logs or any place that looks adventurous for a tiny snail to visit.

2 Use your string to lay out a trail. Get creative with your path. Think about leading a snail over rocks, under logs, or into cracks. Design it like you were making an amazing amusement park adventure for a snail. Here's a pro tip on snails: they can go upside down without any trouble, so don't hold back.

3 Once you have finished, put on your backpack and imagine it is your snail shell. Get down on your belly and follow the trail from start to finish as if you were the snail sliding over and under this wild terrain. Using a magnifying lens will make this journey even more exciting, giving you a close-up view of this microtrek.

4 If you are doing this with a friend, each of you can lay out a trail and then you can swap tracks. Poke tiny sticks into the ground to mark the best parts of your snail-trail adventure.

5 Make a map of it showing all the highlights in your field journal. Name it after some awesome feature.

S N A I L

SNAIL TALES

Before you become a snail, it might be good to know what you are getting yourself into. Snails are soft-bodied animals who tote around a shell. The shells are often quite beautiful and are usually made out of calcium carbonate. Snails cannot leave their shells. If you find a snaillike creature without a shell, it is a snail's close cousin, the slug. Snails have a radical way of eating. Instead of having teeth to rip and shred their food, they have a *radula*, a specialized rough tonguelike organ. It is covered with thousands of microscopic teeth-like structures that scrape the food a snail eats. This scratchy tongue comes in handy for licking up calcium from rocks, soil particles, bones, antlers, and even other snail shells. Snails need to ingest calcium regularly to maintain the strength of their shell as it grows with them.

HUM TO A SNAIL

If you ever see me with an aquatic snail in my hand, chances are I'll be humming to it. I learned a long time ago while on a trip to some tidal pools along the ocean that humming a little tune to a periwinkle, a common type of marine snail, makes something magical happen. Holding the nickel-sized snail in the palm of my hand, I pressed my lips together and offered it a little hummy tune. The snail was tucked away in its shell when I held it, but as I buzzed my song, I felt it stretch its foot out and then watched as its sweet head came out. It trundled around my palm as my purry hum continued.

Ever since then, I've been humming to all the water snails I can find, from the common ocean periwinkle to the small freshwater ones I find down at the beach in my New England town. Sometimes it works and sometimes it doesn't. But when it does work, it is like magic.

THINGS YOU'LL NEED

Aquatic snails

SKILLS YOU'LL LEARN

Handling a wild animal

Showing compassion

Being patient

Experimenting

Observing

1   Find an aquatic snail. You can search for them at the ocean's edge, in rocky tidal pools, in the muck of ponds and lakes, or along the slow-moving edges of streams and rivers.

2   Hold the snail in your hand, gently and low down for its safety. Make sure your hand is wet. Turn the snail so its opening is resting against the center of your palm. Lean your head in so your hum is close to the snail and you can see it and, when and if it comes out, it can see you.

3   Just start humming. You can hum a classic like "Happy Birthday to You" or "Row Row Row Your Boat" or you can freestyle and hum your own tune. You want a soft hum that is full of vibration, one that tickles your lips a bit.

4   Keep humming while you watch. It may take a while, and you might have to try a few snails. Wait for it, and you might feel the slow uncurling of its foot. Look for the head to peek out from the end of the foot. If you are really lucky, you might even get to see it raise its eye stalks as they bend toward you.

5   When you are done, give the snail a thank you, even if it didn't come out to see you, and return it to the water.

DOES HUMMING TO SNAILS REALLY WORK?

Why does humming to a snail seem to make it come out of its shell? It might have something to do with the vibration that humming creates, or maybe it helps the snail feel relaxed in your hand. But some scientists say that humming is just a way for us to pass the time and that eventually, when the snail feels settled, it will emerge anyway. You can conduct your own experiment by repeating the above activity again and again. First find an aquatic snail and hum to it. Have someone be your data collector and write down what happens. Then find another snail and try not humming to it. Record what happens. Repeat this as many times as you want and draw your own conclusions. I don't really care if it works or not. It is still really fun to hum to a snail!

BE A BEACHCOMBER

There are other members of the mollusk club besides snails and slugs that you can be on the lookout for. After arthropods, mollusks are the second largest group of invertebrates. With over eighty-five thousand different species in the world, you might think they'd be as easy to find as ants. But many of these animals are ocean dwellers—clams, mussels, oysters, squid, cuttlefish, and octopuses of the world, to name just a few. A great place to search for them is along the ocean shore. Walking along where the ocean meets the land is always like going on a treasure hunt. Next time you are at the ocean, become a shell seeker.

THINGS YOU'LL NEED : SKILLS YOU'LL LEARN

Things You'll Need	Skills You'll Learn
Field journal	Observing
Pencils	Sorting
Field guide to shells of the area	Comparing
Camera (optional)	Identifying
Magnifying lens (optional)	Describing
Binoculars (optional)	

1   Walk along the ocean shore during low tide. This will give you the best chance to find shells. It's a great place to bring some extra tools for observing, like a magnifying lens, binoculars, and a camera.

2   Many beaches have regulations about collecting shells, so make sure you know the rules before you begin to fill your pockets. Don't worry if you can't bring your treasures home. There are still plenty of ways to enjoy your discoveries, like taking photos, drawing sketches, or writing descriptions in your field journal. If you are collecting shells to bring home, just make sure you are 100 percent positive that your shell is empty of the creature that once lived in it!

3   See if you can sort the shells into groups based on their appearances. What name would you give them? Use a guide to shells and see if you can identify them. Look for the smallest complete shell you can find and the largest. How many different colors can you find of the same type of shell? Do any of your shells look like something ate the soft-bodied animal that lived inside of it? Can you find any that seem like the animal is still inside?

4   Draw a treasure map of your walk and label the spots where you found your favorite shells. Do you notice any patterns in where you are finding the shells? Can you find any other types of animals besides mollusks? How about crustaceans, like crabs, or birds, like gulls? Mark those on your map too.

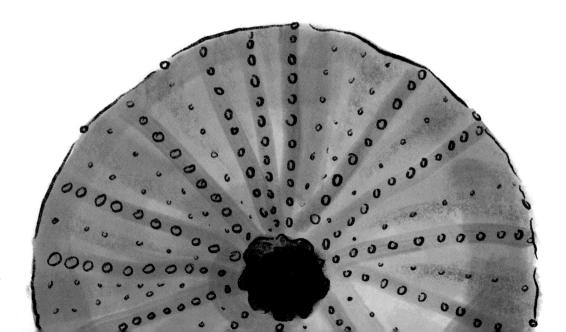

BE A FRESHWATER SHELL SEEKER AND MAKE YOUR OWN VIEW BUCKET

Not everyone lives near the ocean or gets a chance to visit the coast, but don't worry! There are still amazing mollusks to find no matter where you live. North America is actually home to the richest diversity of mussel species in the world, and you can search for them in ponds, lakes, streams, and rivers. You might have to get a bit wet, but it will be worth it to find a few of these shelled creatures.

A fun way to look for them is to use an underwater view bucket, which helps you see down into the bottom of the water. You can buy one or you can make this very easy one.

THINGS YOU'LL NEED

Clear acrylic bucket

Duct tape or electrical tape

Bathing suit or clothes you can get wet

1 You will need a clear acrylic ice or wine bucket, which you can find online for under twenty dollars.

2 Once you have your bucket, you will need to make the sides of it dark or it will be hard to see down into the water. An easy way to do this is to wrap waterproof duct or electrical tape around it. Make sure you tape only the sides, not the bottom.

3 Once the bucket is prepared, take it out for a try. Roll up your pant legs or wear rubber boots or your bathing suit. Hold the bucket by the handles with the opening of the bucket submerged under water and look through the bottom. It's like wearing a snorkel mask without having to put your head into the water. You will get a chance to find mussels and other animals like fish, salamanders, crayfish, dragonfly nymphs, and who knows what else.

REACH FOR THE STARS AND MORE AT THE TIDAL POOL

Have you ever been to a tidal pool? A tidal pool is formed when ocean water gets trapped in a small pocket of land. These special coastal habitats range in size from only a few inches wide and quite shallow to several feet across and a few feet deep. Found usually along rocky coastlines, tidal pools are part of the *intertidal zone*—where the ocean meets the land during high and low tide. Each day when the tide is high, the pool is refilled with water; at low tide, some ocean water remains in the pool, like water in a cup.

Perfect for exploring, tidal pools are like treasure chests of ocean life, filled with spectacular small creatures. From magical sea stars, spiny urchins, and scuttling crabs to hardy ocean snails called periwinkles, a tidal pool offers so much to see. You will never want to leave.

THINGS YOU'LL NEED	SKILLS YOU'LL LEARN
Tide charts (optional)	Observing
Shoes with grippy soles that you can get wet	Touching wild animals
Field journal	Showing compassion
Pencils	Exploring
	Comparing

1   The best time to visit a tidal pool is at low tide. This is when the pools are exposed. Using tide charts for the area where you are visiting will help you and your family figure out when to go. A good resource is the website tide-forecast.com.

2   The rocky shoreline with its tidal pools is a beautiful place to explore but you need to be prepared for the weather and the environment where the ocean meets the land. Check the weather forecast for the shoreline and dress for the conditions. Wearing shoes that you can get wet and that have good grippy treads will keep you from slipping.

3   Once you are at the pool, pay attention to the coast around you. It can be easy to get really focused on the small tidal pool, but it is also important at this habitat to be aware of your surroundings. A couple of good rules for safety include not having the ocean to your back and to pay attention to the time so you know when high tide is coming.

4   Scan the water. Many of these animals are great at camouflaging. They will look like the stones that make up the rocky depression. But look closely. What can you spy? Can you find a sea star or the spiral shell of a periwinkle? What about spiky spines of a sea urchin or barnacles stuck to rocks?

5   Be brave and put your hand in the pool. Does the temperature of the pool surprise you? Let your fingers gently feel the hard shells of the mussels and snails. Be careful not to pry any animals off of the rocks. That is their home, and being stuck like glue on a rock is how they survive the crashing waves at high tide. Can you find anything soft and slippery in the pool, like a fish or a sponge?

6   If you lift up a rock to search for creatures, like crabs, make sure you always return the rock exactly to how you found it. Rocks give these small animals safe hiding spaces from predators, like gulls, and crashing waves at high tide.

7   Use your journal to record the animals you find. Think about how these tidal-pool animals can survive in this extreme environment where waves crash and pulse during high tide and when the tide turns, the pools become still and quiet. If you lived in a tidal pool, what would be your strategy to survive?

8   Remember, what you find at the pool needs to stay at the pool.

VISIT A VERNAL POOL INSTEAD OF A TIDAL POOL

If you don't live near an ocean, visit a vernal pool! A vernal pool is a temporary pond that fills with rainwater and melting snow in the spring and usually dries up by the middle of summer. Similar to tidal-pool animals, animals that live in vernal pools must have special strategies to survive extreme living conditions. Think of these occasional wetlands as big puddles filled with unique wildlife. Since these spring pools are temporary, fish cannot live in them, which gives certain animals like frogs and salamanders a safe place to reproduce and lay their eggs.

FOSSIL FRENZY

Have you ever dreamed of finding a fossil? Or maybe you have already found one. Fossils give you a peek into ancient times. Some of the most common fossils that people find are those of mollusks, their shells pressed forever into rock. Finding one can be hard, or impossible, especially if you don't live in a place that has the type of rocks where fossils formed, like limestone or sandstone. So, while you wait for the next opportunity to go on a fossil expedition, why not make your own fossil? All you need is some clay, a few shells, and plaster of paris, and you won't have to wait for ten thousand years before your fossil is ready.

THINGS YOU'LL NEED	SKILLS YOU'LL LEARN
Paper plate or newspaper	Making
Modeling clay	Designing
Shells	Comparing
Plaster of paris	Observing
Spoon	Creating a model
Field journal	
Pencils	

1   On a paper plate or a piece of newspaper, flatten out a ball of modeling clay. Make it a bit bigger than your shell.

2   Make an imprint of a shell by pressing the side with the most details into the clay. Be careful not to press too hard—you don't want it to go all the way through the clay. You also want the clay to be big enough so that there is some edging around the shell.

3   Carefully remove the shell from the clay. Look to see if it left a clear, deep, and clean impression. If not, roll up the clay, flatten it out, and try again.

THE ANIMAL ADVENTURER'S GUIDE

THE ANIMAL ADVENTURER'S GUIDE

118

4   Once you have the imprint you want, use your spoon to mix up the plaster of paris. Follow the directions on the box.

5   Pour the mixture into the clay and let it harden overnight.

6   Peel away the clay from the hardened plaster. There's your fossil! Look at it and in your journal consider: What details do you see? How does it compare to the actual shell? If you found this fossil, what would you be able to tell about the animal?

FIRST STEPS TO BECOMING A FOSSIL FINDER

Fossils were formed thousands of years ago when plants or animals got trapped in mud or sand. Over time, the remains were covered in more mud and sand, and eventually these layers hardened into stone. Sometimes it wasn't an animal or plant that got trapped but something they left behind, like a footprint, eggshells, a feather, or even poop. Looking at all types of fossils can help tell the story of the past. *Paleontologists* are the scientists who specialize in studying the record of life on Earth through these finds. If you think being one of these scientists sounds interesting, do some exploring in your own neighborhood. Get to know not just the animals that live there now but also the rocks and minerals around you. A paleontologist has to know both!

SLIME TRAIL

SHELLS

WORM

SNAIL

SCAVENGER HUNT: OTHER INVERTEBRATES

You will have to pay attention when searching for worms, snails, slugs, and shells in your neighborhood. Even though these animals don't move very fast, they can be hard to find. Keep your eyes open and your ears tuned in, and try using your imagination too. What can you find from the list below?

* A SILVERY SLIME TRAIL

* WORM POOP

* SOMETHING SLIMY

* SOMETHING THAT WOULD EAT A WORM

* A PLACE WHERE A MUSSEL COULD LIVE

* SOMETHING THAT REMINDS YOU OF A SEASHELL

* THE SOUND OF A WORM, SLUG, OR SNAIL MOVING

* A SPOT TO SEARCH WHERE YOU'D LIKE TO FIND A FOSSIL

* SOMETHING THAT COULD BE YOUR SHELL IF YOU WERE A SNAIL

* ANOTHER ANIMAL WITH TENTACLE-LIKE STALKS

Resources

FOR BIRDS ·

Birds: The Cornell Lab of Ornithology,
www.birds.cornell.edu
Bird descriptions, range maps, photos, and
a vast audio library of bird calls and songs.

Stokes Beginner's Guide to Birds by
Donald and Lillian Stokes
An easy-to-use, color-coded select species
guide perfect for anyone just learning how
to identify birds. Available for both the
Eastern and Western regions of the US.

The Sibley Guide to Bird Life and Behavior
by David Allen Sibley
A thorough and gorgeously illustrated guide
to the birds of North America and their
behavior. Filled with fascinating details about
each bird's life.

*Owling: Enter the World of the Mysterious
Birds of the Night* by Mark Wilson
A wonderful children's guide to owls,
including profiles of owl scientists and
projects, and filled with the author's
incredible photographs.

Pellets Inc., www.pelletsinc.com
A sustainable source of wild but sterilized owl
pellets, available for pellet dissections.

FOR MAMMALS ·

Project Squirrel, https://projectsquirrel.org
Share your squirrel observations to help
scientists and wildlife researchers make
important discoveries about this furry animal.

*Mammal Tracks and Sign: A Guide to
North American Species* by Mark Elbroch
This is a favorite guide with a comprehensive
scat section.

*Peterson Reference Guide to the Behavior
of North American Mammals* by Mark
Elbroch and Kurt Rinehart
Packed with fascinating information and
vividly illustrated with photographs and
sketches of North America's wild mammals.

Roots & Shoots, an initiative of the
Jane Goodall Institute
Visit Jane Goodall's Roots & Shoots webpage
at rootsandshoots.org to find out how Jane is
inspiring the next generation of scientists and
animal lovers.

My Life with Chimpanzees by Jane Goodall
Find how this inspiring animal scientist got
her start and made her discoveries in this
autobiography.

FOR HERPS ·

Calls of Frogs and Toads, https://musicofnature.com/calls-of-frogs-and-toads-of-the-northeast/
Nature recordist Lang Elliott's webpage lets you listen to the different frog calls most often heard in North America and see photos of the frogs that make these amazing sounds.

Seek app
The Seek app, developed by iNaturalist, helps you identify your herp finds from pictures you've taken with your phone.

FrogWatch USA, www.aza.org/frogwatch?locale=en
Participate in the Association of Zoos and Aquariums' FrogWatch USA citizen science program to help scientists collect data on frog populations, diversity, and species accounts.

Matt Patterson Wildlife Artist, Stoneridge Art Studios, mpattersonart.com
Let snake wrangler, amphibian and reptile conservationist, and award-winning artist Matt Patterson's realistic herp art inspire you to draw.

National Audubon Society Field Guide to Amphibians and Reptiles of North America **by John L. Behler and F. Wayne King**
A complete guide to the herps of North America. Includes photos and descriptions. Essential if you are planning on searching for snakes.

FOR ARTHROPODS ·

National Moth Week, http://nationalmothweek.org/
The last full week of July is a celebration of the important ecological role that moths play in our world. Find events and programs here to help you discover the incredible beauty and diversity of these fuzzy flying creatures.

Never Home Alone, www.inaturalist.org/projects/never-home-alone-the-wild-life-of-homes
Upload your arthropod finds into this site and try to identify the creatures using photos on the site.

Kaufman Field Guide to Insects of North America **by Eric R. Eaton and Kenn Kaufman**
A well-laid-out and organized guide to the insects of North America.

Tracks and Sign of Insects and Other Invertebrates: A Guide to North American Species **by Noah Charney and Charley Eiseman**
Want to learn how to identify bug tracks, nests, and holes? Then you will want to look at this unique and thorough guide.

BugGuide, bugguide.net
This handy online bug identification tool even includes a way to identify bug poop, also known as frasse.

FOR OTHER INVERTEBRATES · · · · · · · · · · · · · · · · ·

Wild at Home: Earthworms, www.youtube.com/watch?v=OpbS13JCqv8&list=PLFM-myvMi6E9pjiPsUCGFhSHpDKnX41uOe&index=1
A very short video on what to notice about earthworms.

The Disgusting Critter Series by Elise Gravel
Enjoy these humorous and scientific books by artist and author Elise Gravel highlighting such fascinating creatures as worms and slugs.

The Secret Pool by Kimberly Ridley
This award-winning picture book highlights the unique inhabitants of this temporary wetland while explaining the ecology and cycle of the pool.

National Audubon Society Field Guide to Seashore Creatures: North America by Norman A. Meinkoth
A detailed guide for tidal pooling and beachcombing anywhere in North America.

Seashells: More Than a Home by Melissa Stewart and illustrated by Sarah S. Brannen
Find out all about the seashells and hidden animals that live in them in this nonfiction picture book.

ABOUT THE AUTHOR

If you ask Susie Spikol her favorite animal, she will not be able to choose. She has spent her entire life loving animals, especially the ones that have "bad reputations" like the petite but venomous short-tailed shrew and the famously stinky striped skunk.

As a naturalist at the Harris Center for Conservation Education in a tiny town in New Hampshire, Susie helps people of all ages fall in love with and connect with the natural world. From going on midnight owling expeditions and early morning bird walks to catching frogs and following bear tracks on snowshoes, she spends many of her workdays outside in search of animals and their signs.

Known by some as the Princess of Poop, Susie's award-worthy scat collection has been the talk of her small town when it was once showcased at the town library. When she isn't at work leading people of all ages on nature walks or in her office sorting her scat collection, Susie spends time writing about nature and can be found outside with her three children and two dogs having their own wild adventures. To read more of Susie's writings, find out what she's up to outside, and connect with her about what animals you've been seeing, check out her website at www.susiespikol.com.

Roost Books
An imprint of Shambhala Publications, Inc.
2129 13th Street
Boulder, Colorado 80302
roostbooks.com

Note: It's important to always use your best judgment when interacting with wildlife in nature. Shambhala Publications and the author disclaim any and all liability in connection to the animal activities in this book. Adult supervision is recommended. Always practice caution.

Cover art: Becca Hall
Design by Kara Plikaitis

9 8 7 6 5 4 3 2 1

First Edition
Printed in China

Shambhala Publications makes every effort to print on acid-free, recycled paper.
Roost Books is distributed worldwide by Penguin Random House, Inc., and its subsidiaries.

Library of Congress Cataloging-in-Publication Data
Names: Spikol, Susie, author.
Title: The animal adventurer's guide: how to prowl for an owl, make snail slime, and catch a frog bare-handed—50 activities to get wild with animals / Susie Spikol; illustrated by Becca Hall.
Description: First edition. | Boulder, Colorado: Roost Books, [2022]
Identifiers: LCCN 2021049128 | ISBN 9781611809534 (trade paperback)
Subjects: LCSH: Animals—Study and teaching—Activity programs—Juvenile literature. | Animals—Juvenile literature.
Classification: LCC QL52.55 .S65 2022 | DDC 590—dc23/eng/20211105
LC record available at https://lccn.loc.gov/2021049128